Positive Prejudice as
Interpersonal Ethics

Positive Prejudice as Interpersonal Ethics

Sara Kärkkäinen Terian

LEXINGTON BOOKS
Lanham • Boulder • New York • London

Published by Lexington Books
An imprint of The Rowman & Littlefield Publishing Group, Inc.
4501 Forbes Boulevard, Suite 200, Lanham, Maryland 20706
www.rowman.com

6 Tinworth Street, London SE11 5AL, United Kingdom

British Library Cataloguing in Publication Information Available

Library of Congress Cataloging-in-Publication Data

Library of Congress Control Number: 2020942612
ISBN 978-1-7936-2850-3 (cloth)
ISBN 978-1-7936-2852-7 (pbk)
ISBN 978-1-7936-2851-0 (electronic)

For Camille, Talia, Arthur, and Phoebe

Contents

Preface

To be human is to be in relationships with other humans, and these relationships have a profound effect on our lives. Our attitudes toward others show in our everyday behaviors with or without words, and how a person experiences these interpersonal encounters affects that person's confidence in herself and thus her ability to work toward her goals. Prejudice, the preconceived idea that helps us perceive things, is always there and often shows in undesirable ways—even when no harm is intended.

The above truism has always intrigued me and led me to the study of sociology. This book is an attempt to pull together into a coherent statement some of what I have learned about human interactions in my years of study, life experience, teaching, research, and observations. With it I also attempt to spell out my personal philosophy of interpersonal ethics. My general scholarly orientation is interpretive, nonpositivist, theoretical and qualitative sociology. That orientation acknowledges that total objectivity is impossible, that some interest has led to the choice of a topic in the first place, and then to the type of method chosen. Also, that orientation acknowledges that certain basic assumptions are at the bottom of scientific studies. Personally, I assume that human beings have inherent dignity, that other minds are different from mine, and that people are social and influence one another, thus affecting one another's life experiences.

In my career as a sociologist, I have taught a wide variety of courses at several colleges and universities. As for research, my major interest has always been on interpersonal relationships, especially their ethical dimensions. This book examines the basic philosophy that ran through most of my previous projects. It is not a *magnum opus* but a concise statement of the ideas that I have been researching and working on for decades. It is part of my personal quest to understand people, to see their real essence. It is an attempt to develop a theoretical framework that will combine several areas of inquiry by looking at a deeper level from which the surface level issues emerge. The thesis of this book is that respect for persons means positive prejudice toward them. Combining social psychology with interpersonal ethics, with phenomenology as the foundation, leads to a fresh new approach to the old problem of prejudice.

A personal experience from the beginning of my sociological career may illustrate the question I feel so compelled to explore. When I finished my graduate studies, I was exploring various job opportunities. There was an unexpected opportunity for a newly minted sociologist: the chairman of the architecture department at the university where my husband was teaching had the wonderful insight that architecture students need to learn about the people for whom they design. I set out to learn more about the underlying philosophy in architecture, soon fell in love with the field, and eventually got hired. One day I attended a lecture by the same chairman. He showed slides about a beautiful building. I was greatly inspired and marveled at the beauty architects can conceive.

In the meantime, however, I had signed up for a couple of months' program in an outpatient treatment for alcoholics. Before the architecture opportunity opened up, I had been entertaining the possibility of becoming a counselor in the addictions field, and in preparation decided to go through the program as if I needed it. Actually, I began to identify myself with the participants to the extent that I could say, "I am an alcoholic," because in different circumstances I could have fallen in the same trap. Keeping in mind also that there are different types of addiction—being a workaholic, for example—I could definitely identify. Nevertheless, on the way to the addiction session that same afternoon, after being so inspired by the beauty of architecture, I thought of the contradiction. I wished I could have stayed in the wonder-world of art and architecture; now I was going to deal with ugliness.

The session, however, stopped me in my tracks. As the people opened up and shared their struggles, their desire to clean up their lives—to gain victory over the nasty addiction, and their aspirations for purity and wholeness, I was awed. I felt like each person was a flower opening up to the sun, coming out of the brown earth and presenting a glorious blossom. I felt that no building conceived by architects could match the beauty of human beings who aspire to realize the higher essence of their humanity. Phenomenologically, this beauty of a human soul opened up before me; I beheld it and marveled. It was not the same kind of admiration I had previously had toward a building; this was a living, evolving reality of the inner working of the human spirit. I had previously entertained negative prejudice toward people with addiction problems, now my eyes and heart were opened to see the person behind the problem. My prejudice had turned from negative to positive.

What brought about the transformation? It was the opportunity to participate in a sacred event: human beings opening up the chambers of their hearts—vulnerable, naked, striving to reach up toward a higher realm. It was a precious gift, and it transformed me. Though at the end I did not become an addictions counselor but ended up teaching about human behavior in the architecture and behavioral science departments, the experience has stayed with me as a vivid illustration of the difference between people and things. In essence, this book is about that difference.

As is obvious from the text, my own life experiences have given me many of the insights presented. I am thankful for having had the opportunity to live in several different cultures and to acquire higher education, even though later in life than is usual. And the decades of teaching were an enriching experience, for which I am also thankful. Finally, I want to acknowledge the support and encouragement I have received from several individuals who helped me shape and complete this manuscript. Nancy Johnson read the first chapters and gave important critical feedback that helped sharpen my focus, Linda Lee and Beth Fischer helped with library resources, and conversations with other friends have stimulated my thinking. I am also deeply grateful for the enthusiasm by which the editorial board and my editors at Lexington Books, Courtney Morales and Shelby Russell, have taken up this project, and the encouragement and thoughtful suggestions given by the anonymous reviewer.

My deepest gratitude, however, goes to my husband, Abraham, for not only his encouragement and support through the years and the cross-fertilization of ideas in our "pillow-talks," but also for reading the entire manuscript and giving valuable feedback. Our children Ari, Satu, and Sonia, and their families have been and continue to be the greatest joy in our lives. The book is dedicated to our four grandchildren who have most of their lives ahead of them.

Introduction

The title of this book succinctly spells out its thesis: interpersonal ethics requires an attitude of positive prejudice. The pages that follow are an attempt to analyze and justify that claim on the basis of philosophical and social-psychological theories and studies. Phenomenology provides the foundation for this analysis, and the empirical fields of welfare work and gender and ethnic relations are used as some of the real-life examples. The key terms to be analyzed are "prejudice" and "respect," the latter being at the heart of interpersonal ethics. Books and articles on these topics abound; what new is there to say? My insights come from the intersection of three fields: social psychological studies of interpersonal behavior with focus on prejudice; ethics in terms of respect for persons, that is, how one could improve the social experience of others; and phenomenology of social relations, that is, how one experiences oneself in interpersonal situations, and what types of experiences are empowering. The focus is on face-to-face interpersonal encounters and relationships, though there are implications for group relationships as well.

What makes the difference between positive, uplifting encounters and less positive ones? This is where both phenomenology and ethics enter the picture. Phenomenology examines how people experience the encounters, whereas ethics focuses on what they ought to be like. I am aware of the argument that sociology should stay in the empirical realm and not venture into ethics—at least traditionally, sociologists were expected to merely describe, not prescribe. As Kant and one of his foremost interpreters indicate, "an exclusively empirical philosophy . . . can have nothing to say about morality" (Paton 1964, 8). Such pure empiricism, devoid of ethical concerns, stems from the philosophy of Hume (Ricoeur 1992, 169). Yet American sociology began with moral concerns; the quest to be a science led the discipline away from questions of morality and ethics. The truth is that there is a moral dimension in every social action, thus sociology and moral philosophy cannot be separated (MacIntyre 1984, 72–73). In recent years there has been a definite return in sociology and psychology to discussions of what ought to be, the ideal in social life (e.g., Sayer 2005, 2011; Smith 2003, 2010; Mikulincer and Shaver 2010; Tavory 2011, 272; Stets and Carter 2012; Prasad 2018), and the philosophy of critical realism that is gaining ground in sociology claims that facts and values cannot be separated (López and Potter 2001; Smith 2010; Porpora 2015).

Since this book is an attempt to combine insights from several disciplines, it is not possible to provide an exhaustive literature review of each field. The references are simply to the books and articles that I have come across within my research and have found helpful for my own understanding. With this book I try to show some of the most salient factors that are present in an ethical interpersonal encounter, and explore what respect really means. Writing this book is merely a milepost in my continued effort to figure out what makes supportive relationships, what makes some interpersonal encounters more uplifting and inspiring than others, and what we all could do to steer our dealings with other people in a more positive direction. I hope to outline an ideal that is my goal in my own associations with people.

My approach to the topic is theoretical, or more precisely, phenomenological. Looking at the world phenomenologically means peeling back the layers of socially imposed preconceptions and seeing something with fresh eyes—as if new. This fresh approach, however, does not mean that we gather perceptions into an empty container; our cultural, social and personal backgrounds, interests and such shape our perceptions. Phenomenology examines life as it is lived, not with a detached statistical analysis but with deep penetration into life experience by one who also participates in life. Reasoning in light of philosophical studies further aids understanding. I am especially focusing on three particular empirical problems to illustrate the theory's utility: welfare work, gender, and ethnic relations in terms of prejudice and respect for persons. The examples are from literature, research, and my own observations of everyday life.

With the first two chapters I attempt to provide a context for the theory. The first chapter explains the essentially social nature of the concept of self. This is necessary to establish first because of the highly emphasized individualism in the United States that attributes each person's success or failure to her or his own abilities and efforts alone. While the land of opportunities makes it possible for individuals to function at a higher level and fulfill their dreams, my claim is that the degree to which they are able to do so depends largely on other people's attitudes toward them, the faith others have in them, and the encouragement and moral and other support they receive. Feedback from others plays an important role in shaping people's selves and thus their lives. Phenomenology helps explain how people experience the interactions, while ethics shows what these interactions ought to be like. Thus both have a role in helping us understand the dynamics of interpersonal behavior and factors present in the formation of one's self.

The second chapter will delve more specifically into interpersonal encounters and the dimensions in these encounters that make a difference for better or for worse. Two persons represent two worlds with different histories, cultures, personal orientations, and other background factors that confront each other in each encounter, and the encounters take place in the institutional context of the society with its values and norms. Both cognitive and affective components are present even in brief encounters with strangers as we evaluate and define the situation and act according to these instantaneous definitions. Enduring relationships are also built of separate encounters, thus the same dynamics play a role in them as well. This means that all encounters have a moral weight as they can positively or negatively influence the parties' self-esteem, feelings and motivations. It is in the various encounters between people that attitudes come into play, thus providing the ground on which prejudice rests.

The third chapter then examines the concept of prejudice, its meaning and history, its types and manifestations, and the changing understanding of the concept over centuries. Since prejudice by definition is a prejudgment, present in all our perceptions, the point is not to try to eliminate it but to change it to a positive form. This can happen when a person becomes aware of one's own negatively prejudiced response and is willing to correct it. In addition, by drawing a wider and more inclusive circle that includes those who are different, and by employing the values of kindness and respect, prejudice can be changed from negative to positive. In this light, the challenge is not to get rid of prejudice but to acknowledge one's lack of knowledge about the other person. It also means giving the benefit of the doubt to individuals and communities that we don't know well, acknowledging their contributions to society, and recognizing the inherent value of each human being.

The fourth chapter deals with interpersonal ethics in terms of respect, which obviously is at the heart of positive prejudice. Respect or lack of it shows in our everyday interactions, even in ostensibly innocent remarks. The ethical principle of respect for persons stems from the philosophy of Immanuel Kant who stipulated that each person is to be treated as an end, not merely as a means. While the Enlightenment philosophy fell short of the full implications of universal respect in that it excluded women, minorities, and the colonized, later philosophies have corrected this by emphasizing the need for particular attention to the specific histories, identities, and needs of various previously excluded groups. In other words, particularism is needed for attention to difference, yet such attention is in the context of universalism, understood in a more complete sense.

The fifth chapter provides summaries of the preceding chapters and considers the main concepts, prejudice and respect, from a different angle and with a somewhat critical view. It defines prejudice in general as an attempt to fill in the gap in our insufficient knowledge of the other person and suggests the need to accept that gap and respect the stranger in the status of a stranger, acknowledging our own prejudiced viewpoint and doing our best to stop the process of trying to define the Other. Since positive prejudice could easily be mistaken as blind trust in people we don't know, this chapter also examines the relationship between trust and positive prejudice. With examples, it shows that positive prejudice can include caution and need not mean blind trust in strangers. Overall, ethical encounters focus on the Other and accept our own as well as the Other's "situated understanding" (Sandel 2014). While responding to negatively prejudiced approaches by others presents an additional challenge to those at the receiving end, we all need humility and forgiveness in our interactions, acknowledging that none of us is perfect; at best, we all are "good-ish people" (Chugh 2018).

Theoretically, I have attempted to look at prejudice from an intersection of the separate fields of social psychology, ethics, and phenomenology, and thus contribute to the study of this prevalent social problem. At the practical level, however, the theme of this book may be boiled down to our attitude toward other people that shows in all our everyday interactions and has a weighty effect on the others' self-esteem and ability to work toward their goals. The value of this new analysis of a much-studied attitude, as I see it, is two-fold: by showing how ostensibly unimportant nuances of interpersonal behavior can have weighty effects, it helps us pause and evaluate our interactions; and by suggesting a pathway toward gearing our attitudes in a positive direction, it may motivate us to get on that path. With greater understanding of the phenomenon of prejudice and its place in all our perceptions, we may more honestly see its role in our own behavior and work toward shaping it into a positive form. The aim of our interpersonal behavior will then be the empowerment of others to be the best they can be.

Chapter One

Self as a Social Construct

Prejudice has to do with our attitudes toward other people, and it has definite consequences for the self of the person at the receiving end. That is because human beings are inherently social;[1] our very selves are socially formed and maintained. We are born into a community and become functioning members of the community and the world as a result of interactions with other people. These interactions influence us throughout our lives, and to some extent make us who we are. Although our individualist culture in the Western world emphasizes freedom and independence and holds us responsible for our own lives, the truth is that no person is an island. We human beings shape each other; therefore how we approach other people makes a world of difference in their lives as well as ours.

The social nature of self is the subject of this first chapter. After defining what the concept self means, the focus will be on how the sense of self is developed, maintained, and shaped by social interactions. Whether these interactions are fleeting or part of more enduring relationships, they have the capacity to steer our lives in positive or negative directions. Being fragile, the self experiences a variety of threats in daily life, therefore we each have an ethical responsibility to behave toward others in a way that enhances their experiences in the world and supports their sense of self. Such constructive interactions help create a positive atmosphere for human thriving.

SELF AS ONE'S OWN PERSONHOOD

The idea of self is the central concept of this chapter, but what is self? Definitions abound, and most agree that self is a process though it includes a more stable core. As is well known, Freud believed that human psyche (personality) is basically the unconscious mind that governs behavior, and it consists of three parts: the primitive and instinctual "id" that contains the basic drives, the moral conscience that comes from society that he called "superego," and the self that mediates between the instinctual and moral aspects that he called "ego." Ego is thus the balancing element that keeps mediating between the opposing forces (Freud 1923). Turner (2002, 15) provides the sociological understanding that these parts of self "are not so much entities or structures but processes and phases," formed by interactions and thus constantly reforming by "ego processes."

The early American sociologist George Herbert Mead's idea is somewhat similar to Freud's but focuses more on the cognitive aspect of self. He conceived of the self in two dimensions: the spontaneous, unreflective dimension he termed the "I," and the objective view of oneself he termed the "me." As soon as a person reflects on her spontaneous actions or is aware of her response to stimuli, the self has become "me," an objective understanding of oneself as if looking at oneself with other people's eyes. "The 'I' reacts to the self which arises through the taking of the attitudes of others"—the "me" (1934, 174). Mead notes that we produce the same response in ourselves as in others when we thus see ourselves from the other's viewpoint, yet the "I" is always in the background. In his own words,

> The "I" . . . never can exist as an object in consciousness, but the very conversational character of our inner experience, the very process of replying to one's own talk, implies an "I" behind the scenes who answers to the gestures, the symbols, that arise in consciousness. . . . The self-conscious, actual self in social intercourse is the objective "me" or "me's" with the process of response continually going on and implying a fictitious "I" always out of sight of himself. (Mead 1964, 141)

Thus, according to Mead's theory, there is conversation within the self between its two dimensions, the "I" and the "me." Yet this self has been developed and keeps being developed by our interaction with others; it is not a fixed entity but "essentially a social process going on with these two distinguishable phases" (Mead 1934, 178).

We could say then that self is to be aware of one's own person as an objective entity in the world—existentially separate from others, which means to have a concept or image of oneself. Baumeister (1999) defines a self-concept as "The individual's belief about himself or herself, including the person's attributes and who and what the self is." And Turner (2002, 101) notes that although self is a process, there is a "*core self* or transsituational cognitions and feelings about who a person is" (emphasis Turner's). Thus there is constancy to the concept—because this is who I am, this is how I approach life and do things—that becomes one's identity. Yet the self or identity is not totally static. The philosopher Ricoeur discusses two major meanings of identity: *idem*-identity that implies sameness or permanence, "some unchanging core of the personality," and *ipse*-identity that implies "temporality" and change as "a primary trait of the self." The latter involves "the dialectic of *self* and the *other than self*" (1992, 2–3, emphasis Ricoeur's), an important point for our focus on self as a social construct.

The idea of self includes both a qualitative evaluation of oneself as compared to others and an ideal or goal of what kind of person one would like to be. According to Freud's concept of superego, a person internalizes group expectations and cultural norms and thus creates a conscience and an ego ideal. Turner considers these "the cornerstones of superego processes" that activate emotional responses and thus influence interaction. Ego processes then "create, confirm, and sustain a sexual identity" which is at the core of the general identity in Freud's theory. Interactions that proceed according to expectations result in reinforcing one's identity (Turner 2002, 15).

Thus there is no isolated self; the Other is necessary for the development of one's self, one's consciousness, one's own view of one's personhood, and the kind of person one is. But who is this "me" that responds to the stimuli and whom I see as myself and whom others see? What does it mean to be a person? In his book *What Is a Person?* Christian Smith provides a comprehensive definition of a person and introduces dimensions that will be discussed extensively in this book:

> By *person* I mean a conscious, reflective, embodied, self-transcending center of subjective experience, durable identity, moral commitment, and social communication who—as the efficient cause of his or her own responsible actions and interactions—exercises complex capacities for agency and intersubjectivity in order to develop and sustain his or her own communicable self in loving relationships with other personal selves and with the impersonal world. (Smith 2010, 61)

The theories discussed above imply the conscious and reflective nature of self. Though the self is embodied, "the body is not a self, *as such*, but becomes a self only when it imagines itself in relation to others; without social experience, therefore, the self cannot develop" (Rieff 1970, xix, emphasis his). Yet embodiment is implied in seeing oneself as others see us; self is not a spirit floating in the air but is embodied in physical existence and actual empirical situations (Dorothy Smith 1987). The durable identity refers to the constancy in the self-concept, and transcending self is inherent in the social nature of self. I shall discuss social communication below and the moral commitment a bit later.

The above definition also states that a person is "the efficient cause" of his or her actions and interactions and "exercises complex capacities for agency." Having agency means the power and capacity to make decisions, to be in control of one's life, and to work toward achieving one's own goals. Agency is often discussed in its relationship to social structure—the norms and institutions that regulate social life. This relationship, in the words of Cole, is "an ever-evolving dialectic" in that each influences the other and thus change in one requires change in the other. Both individual agency and the collective agency of groups can either "reaffirm social order by reproducing the norms and existing social relationships, or it may serve to challenge and remake social order by going against the status quo to create new norms and relationships." Such "remaking" can involve various forms of resistance or simple acts like demanding respect (Cole 2020).

But the complex concept of agency means even more: agency has both a temporal and a relational component in that past development, future aspirations, and the present social context are interwoven with a personal capacity, indeed are integral parts of it. Social movements like the recent "Black Lives Matter" movement are examples of this. At the individual level, autonomous, competent adult human beings have agency,[2] and it is developed and maintained in relationships with others (Emirbayer and Mische 1998; Kundu 2017). In fact, agency is needed to have a quality called "grit"—determination and perseverance to make something of one's life, thus agency is more fundamental than grit though the latter is emphasized a great deal (Duckworth 2016). All these dimensions are embedded in the social world that forms and maintains our agencies, our very selves.

THE SOCIAL SHAPING AND MAINTENANCE OF SELF

To begin with, a child is born into a community and from the first breaths inherits the cultural context of that community. Thus

> selfhood begins not with the philosophical hubris that the subject is an autonomous self but with an awareness that the subject enters consciousness already formed by the symbolic systems within its culture. Consciousness is never independent or empty—a tabula rasa—but always already interpenetrated by the founding symbols and stories that constitute one's communal heritage. (Wallace 2002, 81, about Ricoeur)

In this ready symbolic universe, the development of self begins as a baby learns to identify himself as separate from other people and learns the specifically human qualities. A few cruel cases of severe social neglect of normal children are instructive: though fed, without social interaction these children became *feral* (untamed) and acted more like wild animals than human beings (Malson 1972; McClean 1978; Shattuck 1980; Hopkins 1983). They could not speak and had trouble with reading emotional languages as well (Turner 2002, 80). A child becomes a functioning human being and a unique personality within her culture through socialization, a process through which she not only learns human behavior and the specific features of her culture but also develops her self-esteem and confidence in her abilities—her agency—as she receives the encouragement and support of others around her.

According to the psychologist Eric Erikson, this is the stage in which the child develops basic trust that provides "a rudimentary sense of ego identity" (1963, 247). Similarly, Honneth (1996) shows that the importance of recognition begins at this stage as the child's basic needs and need for love are fulfilled, that someone recognizes these needs and responds to them. Then in the ongoing socialization, parents, siblings, friends, teachers, and other significant people all participate in the social construction of the child's self. That self provides a solid foundation to build on as the child grows into adulthood and sets his goals for life.

While the self-concept formed in childhood is most crucial, growing into adulthood is by no means the end of the social construction of self. Self-esteem and confidence need to be socially maintained for one's entire life, lack of such maintenance can erode them. Putting Freud's theory into a more sociological framework, influenced by Mead, Turner writes:

> When interaction is nonproblematic, ego interprets the gestures of alters as communicating positive sentiments that, in turn, increase the likelihood that id impulses will be consummated, that identity will be reinforced, and that commitments to group expectations, goals, and ideals as well as cultural standards have been demonstrated. A lifetime during which interaction has followed this cycle will produce emotionally healthy and socially adjusted individuals. (Turner 2002, 15)

In his sociological summary of "Freud's First Principles of Interaction," Turner (2002, 16) emphasizes positive and affirming responses from others as necessary for the healthy development and maintenance of self. Social uprooting that makes one a stranger often deprives a person of such feedback, as is the case for women who follow their husbands' careers, resulting in the disintegration of their lifeworlds "into a collection of episodes" that is not organized by one's own experience and lacks a "biographical anchorage of the self in present witnesses to the individual past" (Dorothy Smith 1987, 96).

There are personality differences, however, as to how much other people influence our self-concepts (Ebren 2009); those with a greater degree of confidence may depend less on others' encouragement and support, but even the most confident individuals are affected by feedback from others. The feedback may be as subtle as unspoken expectations that convey trust in the person. Experiencing a sense of trust makes a person feel included and verifies self and identity, resulting in positive emotions (Turner 2002, 131); furthermore, knowing that an important person believes in your abilities increases intrinsic motivation (Wheeler et al. 1978, 140–143) because it increases self-confidence. "The soft bigotry of low expectations," on the other hand, easily leads to self-doubt and thus low achievement. The famous Rosenthal experiment on the effect of teacher expectations on children's success in school is one example that shows how the children's performance was much better when the teacher believed that they were smart (Rosenthal and Jacobson 1968; Rosenthal 2003).

Social scientists and philosophers have offered multiple theories of the ways this social influence shapes our personalities. It is not necessary to review all these theories here; a brief glance at a couple of classical sources shows the picture. More than a century ago, Cooley (1902) developed his theory of the "looking-glass self." Simply put, this depicts society as a mirror that reflects to us an image of ourselves. As we observe others' reactions to our behavior, we not only adjust our behaviors accordingly but also gradually form our self-concepts on the basis of that feedback. For example, your self-concept as a kind and capable person—perhaps one who solves others' problems—has been shaped by such a mirror image. You have been commended for your kindness and problem-solving ability, so you have come to define yourself with these characteristics.

Mead (1934) elaborated on Cooley's theory by pointing out the symbolic nature of human interactions. Words are symbolic too, but you may not even need them to get the feedback: people's symbolic gestures or expressions (frowns, smiles, shrugs, etc.) show you whether they appreciate your helpfulness—which reinforces your positive self-concept—or whether they see your intended help as meddlesome, wishing to push you aside like a small child may do when she wants to tie her own shoes. This feedback helps you adjust your behavior and your self-concept. Approval and disapproval are easy to read in expressions; in fact, Turner (2002) sees visual communication as more basic for humans than verbal communication. All in all, multiple research studies continue to show how people influence one another in various ways (e.g., Manning, Pogson, and Morrison 2008; Knobloch and Schmelzer 2008; Aviram 2009; Mikulincer and Shaver 2010), thus the faith an individual has in herself is largely based on her perception of the faith others have in her.

In his definition of personhood quoted above, Christian Smith sees "social communication" as an integral part of it. Social communication, of course, does not mean only the individual's communication to the outside world but also the communication one receives, what one infers from it. Thus even our subjective experiences and durable identities are socially constructed and maintained. This interchange constitutes the social construction of the self. There is no self, no person—even no reality—without community, as Berger and Luckmann assert in their classic book *The Social Construction of Reality*. These authors claim that our knowledge of things is based on a specific social context; others with a different context "know" the same things quite differently. Our concepts of self, how we "know" ourselves, our identities, are socially constructed as well. "Like all subjective reality, [our identity] stands in a dialectical relationship with society" and "is formed by social processes. Once crystallized, it is maintained, modified, or even reshaped by social relations" (1967, 173).

The development and maintenance of a healthy self-image also requires recognition by others, which is a basic human need. The historical figure most connected with the recognition theory is Hegel. Later Levinas and Ricoeur found in it an answer to the alienation that people felt with increasing industrialization and urbanization (Sohn 2014). Since the 1990s, philosophers have discussed the concept more extensively (e.g., Taylor 1992; Honneth 1996, 2012; Fraser and Honneth 2003; Ricoeur 2005) because lack of recognition is an increasing problem in today's urban world. In his definitive work on the subject, Honneth (1996) identifies three separate spheres in which human beings need recognition. As mentioned above, the first sphere is in infancy when the child's basic needs and especially the need for love are recognized. When these needs are satisfactorily fulfilled, the child develops self-confidence and secure primary relationships. The second sphere centers on rights, especially legal rights as a citizen. When a person is thus legally recognized and has rights such as voting rights, she gains self-respect. The third sphere refers to being recognized and valued in a community for one's specific qualities and contributions, for having social value and solidarity in the community. That results in healthy self-esteem that facilitates self-actualization.

Lack of recognition, on the other hand, can hinder a person's self-actualization, as (Iser 2013) explains: "those who fail to experience adequate recognition, that is, those who are depicted by the surrounding others or the societal norms and values in a one-sided or negative way, will find it much harder to embrace themselves and their projects as valuable. Misrecognition thereby hinders or destroys persons' successful relationship to their selves." In other words, faith in ourselves, in our abilities and our projects, requires constructive feedback and recognition from others. In Turner's words (2002, 112), one's "core self" needs to be confirmed by others.

In short, other people have a lot to do with one's self-image, thus each person affects the self-image of others. If the feedback from those around us is mostly affirming, our agency is strengthened and we feel energized to work toward our goals. Negative feedback or lack of meaningful feedback may lead to self-doubt that lowers one's self-esteem and the value one places on oneself. Self is fragile and dependent on affirmation from others. This is especially a challenge for people who move alone into a new community where they are not known, or a new country where the culture with its symbols may be somewhat if not mostly different. It is also a challenge for minority groups that are often looked down upon by the majority. Recognition theory shows the harmful effects of the lack of verification of one's self.

EXPERIENCING SELF IN INTERACTIONS

How we ought to treat other people is one thing—to be discussed in the next section on ethics—but how we experience the social interactions is another. The latter is a subject that belongs to phenomenology, so a little introduction to that school of thought is in order. Simply put, phenomenology is the study of phenomena—things that appear to the senses or that people experience. This philosophy differs from ontology, which focuses on the existence of things independent of perception, and the order and structures of that reality. For phenomenology, reality is seen only through the lived experience of an experiencing subject; what is important is that these phenomena exist in the perceiving person's experience, and the investigations describe the reality that the perceiving person is experiencing. For that reason, phenomenology addresses our concern here of how the subjective self experiences social encounters either as threats to self or as affirmations of self.

Husserl, the founder of this school of thought in its modern form, focused initially on transcendental phenomenology, on "pure" consciousness, not on the natural or even the social world. Alfred Schutz, however, developed his "psychology of pure intersubjectivity" (Schutz 1967, 44)—how people experience the world in similar ways or at least try to understand each other when there are differences—something that he said social scientists take for granted (Schutz 1970, 55). Schutz sought "to anchor an analysis of consciousness and experience in the exchange of significant signs or gestures" (Turner 2002, 9), that is, in cognitive interaction. For him, better understanding of human beings can be attained "in face-to-face encounter, in interpersonal relationship, in 'dialogue,' in 'commitment'" (Walsh 1967, xv), in a "we-relation" which means "living" in it, being absorbed in common experiences. Schutz and Luckmann (1973, 64) explain the importance of face-to-face interaction for understanding others as follows: "The more I give myself over to reflection, the less I live in the common experience and the more distant and mediate is my consociate. The Other whom I experienced immediately in the we-relation becomes in reflection the Object of my thought."

Dorothy Smith (1987, 126) refers to "Schutz's cognitively-based conception of social reality" as requiring "mysterious 'idealizations' of intersubjectivity," and she emphasizes the need to look at the ongoing social reality rooted in actual activities of subjects, including their embeddedness in oppressive social relations. Such oppression definitely influences social relations, but for our context here Schutz and Luckmann provide a valuable insight: merely thinking about the other in place of joining in common experiences with him is objectification, which I will discuss below as a threat to self.

Several other philosophers—for example, Heidegger, Merleau-Ponty, Marcel, Ricoeur, and the latter Husserl—have attested "that consciousness, bounded temporally, finds itself already always included in an intersubjective world" (Muldoon 2002, 16). In his preface to Merleau-Ponty's *Phenomenology of Perception*, Landes writes:

> The phenomenological world is not pure being, but rather the sense that shines forth at the intersection of my experiences and at the intersection of my experiences with those of others through a sort of gearing into each other. The phenomenological world is thus inseparable from subjectivity and inter-subjectivity, which establish their unity through the taking up [*la reprise*] of my past experiences into my present experiences, or of the other person's experience into my own. (Landes 2012, lxxxiv)

Phenomenology of the social world shows a multitude of nuances present in our interpersonal association. When we face another human being, we do so with a "natural attitude" (Schutz), which means that we take for granted the existence of the other person, as we take for granted that the objects we see actually exist. But as chapter 3 in this book will show, this "natural attitude" also involves the prejudices that our culture and personal preferences present to the encounter. We organize the world by typifications, classification schemes that assign not only things but also people into categories, be they ethnic, religious, occupational, or something else. These "typificatory schemes" enter our interpersonal relationships as well (Berger and Luckmann 1967, 31–34). Aside from their positive roles that help us order the universe, these classifications can easily become stereotypes (discussed in chapter 3). These are some of the dimensions of intersubjective experiences.

Objectification

How, then, do our interpersonal experiences sometimes become threats to self? One problem is objectification, which may not look bad on the surface but results in negative feelings in the person thus objectified because it makes her a "thing." To make another person merely an object of my actions—even charitable ones—or to make her an instrument for my purposes, to use her, is to make her a thing and deny her personhood. Being a subject means that she is different from me, and she has her own ideas and goals. Notice that subjective experience is at the center of Christian Smith's definition of a person, quoted above. To assume that the other person's purposes coincide with mine is to deny her agency, her humanness. Sometimes even a tongue-in-cheek humorous statement can inadvertently make the other person an object, like in a mattress commercial on television a woman says: "It's the best thing I have in my house," and then adds with a chuckle, "except for my husband." Humor aside, too often in everyday communication people are inadvertently treated as things; that is objectification that results in a threat to self.

A multitude of examples could be given from the field of ethnic relations. There was a time in the United States when some individuals from minority groups were displayed in county fares for people to view—like zoo animals (Keller 2006), not to speak of them being sold in the marketplace. Other societies are not exempt from similar sins. At present, objectification of minorities is subtler in the western world, but it still exists all over the globe. For a milder example of objectification, people often express curiosity when for the first time they meet a person from a given culture, as if to put a checkmark on their list that they have met someone from such a country or place of origin. While curiosity may be an innocent desire to know, it may be focused more on oneself than the other person, and that makes its effect on the other person more complicated.

Curiosity was originally directed toward strange objects or novel experiences that inspired travel—and it is vital for scientific discovery (Leslie 2014), but the Enlightenment with its "new science of man" made human beings its objects. Pairing curiosity with "its cousin-passions in wonder and amazement," Rousseau writes: ". . . curiosity had been so far transformed from its early footing in marvels of the natural and artificial world that by 1751 it routinely begins to apply to *modern persons* and their sexual wonder" (Rousseau 2006, 215–217). Curiosity definitely has a positive function and is key to acquiring knowledge, but it makes a difference what its object is.

Today curiosity even toward other people is usually seen positively, yet there is a fine line between mere curiosity and genuine interest: curiosity aims at filling one's felt "information gap" (Loewenstein 1994, 93), whereas interest focuses on the other person for his own sake and thus is different from a restless need to know some trivial fact. The other person, especially if he frequently experiences people's curiosity, may feel objectified because rather than being seen as a unique person he has become a specimen or type, functioning to add to someone's stereotypical "knowledge." Genuine interest in another person strengthens that person's sense of self, whereas mere curiosity involves a danger of making the person an object that is a threat to self.

Women often experience objectification because of their gender, whether in public, in the workplace or home, or in the sexual sphere. Beauty contests objectify the contestants because the attention is mainly on physical attributes; the talent show still remains secondary. And when women don't get credit for teamwork or housework, their work is taken for granted and they are being used, thus objectified. This is what Dorothy Smith (1987, 83) means with her observation that women "liberate men into abstraction" by doing the concrete work so men can engage in intellectual pursuits. This situation is similar to the well-known insight of Karl Marx that sees workers in the capitalistic system as commodities, whose work benefits others and not them.

Objectification of women in the sexual sphere is widespread. Instances of it would make a long list: a man whistling at a pretty woman, conquests to satisfy a man's sexual needs, prostitution, etc. But objectification can also take place in love relationships. In an article on sexual objectification, Martha Nussbaum (1995, 249) quotes Andrea Dworkin from *Woman Hating* (1974): "It is true, and very much to the point, that women are objects, commodities, some deemed more expensive than others—but it is only by asserting one's humanness every time, in all situations, that one becomes someone as opposed to something. That, after all, is the core of our struggle."

Even romantic love can be love of the other as an object based on the lover's needs. Kierkegaard (1995) writes that erotic love is selfish, pagan, perhaps because with its passion it often objectifies the Other. One such example is in an 1874 novel by Thomas Hardy, *Far from the Madding Crowd*. Bob Boldwood was desperately "in love" with Bathsheba Everdene, though in an idealized sense since he had only "occasional observation of her from a distance, and the absence of social intercourse with her." The 41-year-old bachelor sought out the much younger Bathsheba and made a desperate proposition of marriage, pleading, "My life is a burden without you"—only eliciting her sympathy. The novelist wisely concludes: "The rarest offerings of the purest loves are but a self-indulgence, and no generosity at all" (Hardy, 1993, 97, 99, 101).

Such love toward an object is "monological" rather than "dialogical" because it "is not conceived of as shared action and feeling" (Krebs 2010, 28). Moreover, as Hardy (1993, 102) further concludes, it seeks to "possess" the loved one: "It appear that ordinary men take wives because possession is not possible without marriage, and that ordinary women accept husbands because marriage is not possible without possession; with totally differing aims the method is the same on both sides." In other words, men need marriage to gain a property, and women pay for marriage by becoming a property. That is objectification in a graphic sense, fortunately not as common today in the Western world as in the 19th century when Hardy wrote his novel.

Perhaps "love at first sight" often includes such objectification. Though it could mean detecting a soul mate, without mutuality it can be merely a distant admiration where the other doesn't exist as a subject but as an object of one's gaze or yearning. It can make the loved one inanimate, a thing, an object of reflection—as Schutz and Luckmann (1973, 64, quoted above) explained. Krebs further discusses the importance of mutuality: "When analyzing romantic love and friendship, we should start with the sentence 'two people love each other', and not with 'A loves B'" which focuses on individual emotions. With the latter "we can perhaps explain the beginning of love, the falling in love, with its, often intense, yearning for closeness, or also unrequited love, but not love proper" (2010, 29). Discussing Martin Buber's *I and Thou* (1970), the British writer M. M. Owen (2018) comments:

> Falling in love is partly the terrifying realisation that you have stepped into reciprocity; that someone is now able to cause you terrible pain. This is the cost, the gamble. As Buber said, love "without real outgoing to the other . . . love remaining within itself—this is called Lucifer." A love that can't travel is the love of a narcissist. A life immersed exclusively on the I-It is the life of a sociopath.

It is obvious that love in its truest sense does not objectify the loved one but affirms her. That, however, requires mutuality that Krebs (2010) calls "dialogical love."

Classic discussions on love and friendship provide foundational insights. Nussbaum discusses the difference between *eros* and *philia*, the latter being Aristotle's term for love. She states, "the emphasis of *philia* is less on intensely passionate longing than on disinterested benefit, sharing, and mutuality; less on madness than on a rare kind of balance and harmony" (1986, 354). As Aristotle emphasizes, *philia* involves mutual interests, activities, and mutual respect for one another. Although, according to the philosopher Konstan (2008), the exact meaning of *philia* is still a matter of debate, "it is unequivocally and emphatically altruistic" in that "one wishes and acts to realize good things for the other's sake, in accord with what the other conceives as good." Love and friendship, then, "are best understood . . . as an altruistic desire which, when reciprocated, results in a state of affairs that Aristotle, and Greeks in general, called *philia*" (Konstan 2008, 209, 212). Such altruism and mutuality are strong antidotes to objectification.

With mutuality and respect, objectification does not happen. That is the idea in Levinas's (1998) emphasis on the radical otherness of the other—that means even a sexual partner, in which case we need "the capacity to tolerate differences with generosity" (deBotton, 2016)—and that the other is a neighbor. A neighbor does not exist for my sake but alongside, in his own right and with his own life and identity. According to Heidegger's (1962, 80) existential phenomenology, we "reside alongside" the world and must have an attitude of care and responsibility toward the world; this means toward other people too.

Often, however, even ostensibly kind and caring interactions can be experienced negatively, depending on diverse factors. For example, psychologists Firestone and Catlett (2009, xvii) discuss the "toxic character traits that injure other people's self-esteem." They list superiority, domineering, intrusiveness, and "martyred or victimized orientation" as some of those traits. Superiority sometimes takes the form of paternalism, one-upmanship, people pleasing, or sanctimonious behavior. However praiseworthy such behaviors may appear on the surface, they are self-centered; they are vices because they objectify the other (and maybe oneself) and can kill the other's initiative and motivation, thus hampering her quest for personhood. These are the risks of "do-goodism" that Christian Smith (2010) discusses.

Other Threats to Self

Turner introduces several other processes that result in threats to self. Applying Freud's theory to interaction, he observes that ego's efforts "to integrate impulses (id) with internalized standards of groups and culture (superego) and with self-definitions (sexual identity)," in problematic situations "often lead to negative emotional responses from others, thereby setting off new sociodynamic cycles that potentially can cause pathology and maladjustment." This happens when "individuals interpret others' signals as not accepting their behaviors as appropriate or competent." In an effort to sustain self, a person in such situations employs defense mechanisms, such as repression, displacement, or projection. Among other negative outcomes, such interactions can result in "self-doubts about who one is." As Turner observes further, interaction for Freud is an emotionally laden process, and the emotions received from others are the most significant in that they can block individuals' "ability to meet their needs," "manage negative feelings," and "sustain a stable identity" (Turner 2002, 15, 17–18). Threats to self are a source of defense mechanisms, and these defense mechanisms bring more negative emotions from others, thus possibly escalating to more serious problems, such as lack of inclusion, even ostracization that "makes it difficult to get back into people's good graces" and may lead the person to anger and depression (Turner 2002, 90–91, 130). This shows the importance of gearing interactions in a positive direction from the start.

Phenomenology helps us understand how people experience interactions and how these interactions affect self, the sense of agency, motivation, and faith in one's abilities. Problematic interactions threaten the sense of self, whereas recognition and appreciation by others strengthen it. The real meaning of social behavior is often far below the surface-level words or expressions. To approach another person with that person's best in mind is a fine art.

CONSTRUCTIVE INTERACTIONS

Thinking about how we ought to approach other people takes us to the realm of ethics. To clarify the terms, "ethics" and "morality" are often used interchangeably, and according to Ricoeur they are basically the same, one stemming from Greek and the other from Latin—both referring to *mores*. Fraser, however, separates the two, pairing justice—understood as "the right"—with morality, and achieving "the good" as the domain of ethics (Fraser and

Honneth 2003, 27–28). Ricoeur, too, reserves the term ethics to the aim of achieving the good (the teleological perspective that stems from Aristotle), and morality to the norms that spell out the obligations and constraints (the deontological perspective that stems from Kant). He clearly prefers the former and sees ethics as encompassing morality (Ricoeur 1992, 170). This distinction and preference for ethics suits the purpose here as well since the focus of this book is on achieving the good in interpersonal relationships more than on the rules for such conduct. The Kantian perspective, however, also gives important insights for this purpose, as will be seen in chapter 3.

Another school of ethics that has been revived in recent years is virtue ethics. This is based on the classical virtues: wisdom, justice, courage, and temperance. Siding with the Stoic understanding, you cannot have only one or only some of them but need them all; you need wisdom to know what is just or right, courage to act upon it, and temperance to know where to draw the line. The focus is on the moral character of the acting person rather than on rules or obligations. To elaborate on the above-given example of helpfulness, a good person will help, but even a better person will consider what is best for the other rather than reinforcing her self-concept as a helpful person. Representing that school of thought, Christian Smith prioritizes the good over the right. "Within that framework, I argue that the good for human persons is to flourish as persons, to realize our own nature, to develop in fullness what we actually are" (Smith 2010, 385). Similarly, MacIntyre observes that

> there is a fundamental contrast between man-as-he-happens-to-be and man-as-he-could-be-if-he-realized-his-essential-nature. Ethics is the science which is to enable men [*sic*] to understand how they make the transition from the former state to the latter. Ethics therefore in this view presupposes some account of potentiality and act, some account of the essence of man [*sic*] as a rational animal and above all some account of the human *telos*. (MacIntyre 1984, 52)

This perspective, based on Aristotle's *Nicomachean Ethics*, is both teleological and virtue-based—a good person does the right thing and in a way that brings good consequences, such as empowering others to realize their best potential.

Care ethics is a more recent theory of ethics, first introduced as a theory by Carol Gilligan (1982) in her book *In a Different Voice*. In a more recent interview (Webteam 2011), Gilligan described care ethics as a "different voice" because it "joined self with relationship and reason with emotion." Furthermore, it "starts from the premise that we are inherently relational, responsive beings and the human condition is one of connectedness or interdependence." We are "hard-wired for cooperation." Everyone should have a voice and should be listened to with respect. Because of its initial context of gender relations, from the patriarchal viewpoint care ethics is considered a feminist theory. Its goal, however, is to promote human flourishing in general, and virtue means striving for that goal in a way that avoids extremes while empowering others. The theory is normative; a morally right action "is to help individuals achieve a basic level of social functioning" (Nussbaum 2000, 72). This basic level includes faith in oneself so one can work toward one's goals, and that faith is acquired in respectful encounters with others. Respect includes trust in people's ability to soar once opportunities are available. Such empowerment is also the theme of Paulo Freire in his *Pedagogy of the Oppressed* (1970).

Ethics, by definition, deals with how we ought to behave in order to enhance human well-being and maximize the realization of human potential, whereas phenomenology—discussed above—describes how each of us experiences our encounters. Often these two philosophies are not discussed together, but one philosopher who has done so is Emmanuel Levinas. In several works, he has combined ethics and phenomenology in his examination of the face-to-face encounter. For example, in *Humanism of the Other* (2003) he describes how the other confronts us as a Face—naked, vulnerable, open, pleading, "Please don't kill me." Such vulnerability is present in most interpersonal encounters, thus how we approach this "naked" face makes a world of difference. Most of us are not literally intending to kill the other, so what does Levinas mean? Perhaps the "killing" is the destruction of the other's self-esteem as a result of being ignored, despised, looked down upon, objectified, or spoken to with unkind words. Conversely, an uplifting encounter energizes the other and thus is life-giving.

A major theme in Levinas's philosophy is that we exist totally for the sake of the other. "I am in myself through the others" and "I exist through the other and for the other" (Levinas 1991, 112, 114); the other has moral priority over our selves. He doesn't show, however, what to do when the other takes advantage of one's self-sacrifice. That is what Brené Brown (2015, 122–23, 127–28) means by her observation that generosity needs boundaries; while extending generosity we should not lose our integrity, which means holding both ourselves and others accountable. Furthermore, Levinas does not account for the problem of pushing help when the other doesn't want it. Not every "other" is a needy person! Pushing help when it is not needed is not ethical; it is a position of superiority, one of the "toxic" character traits discussed above.

Not every philosopher agrees with Levinas's seemingly one-sided emphasis. Ricoeur, for example, points out that one must have a self before one can understand one's duty toward the other and be able to respond to the call for help. Ricoeur "successfully mediates the dialectic between self-esteem and solicitude for others in his ethical thought," and "stubbornly insists on preserving self-love and other-regard in a correlative tension" (Wallace 2002,

80, 86). Once on the radio a man described how he always felt that he was "not good enough." As a result of counseling he acquired some self-esteem and concluded that "now I can love." You can love others when you are secure about yourself; you are not worried about losing yourself because your feet are on solid ground. Furthermore, as Levinas also notes, the other does not necessarily have needs that I can fill; the desire for others is "sociality" (Levinas 2003, 29). Both parties may be competent and self-sufficient, but it is in human nature to desire company, and appropriate self-love is a prerequisite for truly loving others.

Let us briefly view an example from another social arena: welfare work toward the economically disadvantaged. Helping the less fortunate is an ethical obligation, but how it is done makes a big difference. Much of it is done for selfish reasons, to be a good Christian, a good citizen, whatever. Obviously in that case the focus is not on the needy person but on the self of the helper. Such approach uses the recipient for upgrading one's image in one's own eyes as well as in the eyes of others, and using another human being is objectification in that she or he becomes a tool or a thing. Other times the helper does focus on the recipient but from a superior position, becoming—as Luther says—like God to the needy person. Only when the recipient is seen as a neighbor is there respect and mutuality. One study identified four different motivations or themes for religious welfare work: do-goodism, obligation ethic, love ethic, and justice ethic (Terian 1984). Obviously the first two focus on the self of the helper; the last two are more ethical because they respect the recipient. This will be discussed more in a later chapter.

The point is that when duality and intersubjectivity are not present, one or the other of the parties disappears. According to Levinas (1987, 41), in knowledge "the object is absorbed by the subject and duality disappears," and in ecstasy "the subject is absorbed in the object and recovers itself in its unity." And he concludes: "All these relationships result in the disappearance of the other." An expression of love based on one's own needs is not an exercise of kindness, as Hardy (quoted above) observes, whereas "The desire for Others—sociality—arises in a being who lacks nothing" (Levinas 2003, 29). The object then is companionship, not possession of the other.

A "sympathetic emotional engagement" (Lawrence-Lightfoot 1999, quoting Harris 1997), different from our dealing with objects, is an integral part of interpersonal attitudes. There is considerable disagreement whether a positive emotion toward others should be sympathy or empathy, and sometimes definitions overlap. Sympathy—the older of the two terms—literally means feeling with, but has acquired a more specific feeling of sorrow or pity for someone who is experiencing hardship or grief (e.g., sympathy cards for someone who has lost a loved one). "Sympathy consists of feelings of sorrow or concern for the distressed or needy other" (Eisenberg 2010, 130). In his *The Nature of Sympathy* (1913), Max Scheler (1913/1970) distinguishes four forms of sympathy: joint feeling; sympathy "about something," like joining with others in their joy or sorrow; emotional infection; and emotional identification, "a borderline case of infection in which one self absorbs another" (Krebs 2010, 13, summarizing Scheler). The second meaning, sharing another person's joy or sorrow, is the most usual understanding of sympathy.

Empathy, on the other hand, has a more cognitive dimension, as in "Understanding the internal experience of another person" (Siegel and Hartzell 2003, 224). Feelings, however, are present also in some of the definitions: "feeling as the other person feels" (Batson 2010, 20) or "feeling into," taking another person's viewpoint (Howe 2013, 9), putting oneself in the shoes of another. Firestone and Catlett discuss empowerment from empathy; but "giving sympathy and arousing sympathy in another person are damaging to self and others in that they reinforce victimized thinking" (2009, 244). And according to Brené Brown (2015, 156), sympathy is "a form of disconnection" whereas "empathy is the heart of connection." Many others (e.g., Meyers 1993) agree, placing empathy over sympathy. Other commentators, however, feel that sympathy and compassion are preferable because empathy can be "distorting, controlling, presumptuous, and paternalistic" (Engster 2007, 197–98; see also White 2000, 113–14, 121, and Noddings 2002, 13–14). A person saying, "I know how you feel," may not know at all.

In recent years empathy seems to have become a buzzword in Silicon Valley, and some feel that it is a dispassionate approach toward other people that in the final analysis is used manipulatively for one's self-interest, a useful tool for marketing (Hess 2016). Schutz sees empathy as impossible because it is impossible to fully enter another person's mind and experiences (Schutz 1967, 115). According to him, one can never fully understand another person, can never really step in his shoes; to even postulate such a goal is absurd—and Levinas agrees (quoted above). Because each person's experience has been different, and each person has a different stock of knowledge, each person experiences even the supposedly same thing differently. We can only acknowledge the simultaneity; that is, we can experience something at the same time, and in so doing we are growing older together, aging together. But what this simultaneous experience means to each is different; only the factual event—such as watching a bird in flight (Schutz's example)—is the same. Another criticism of empathy sees it as insufficient explanation of our concern for others because we are embedded a priori with others in the world; empathy merely makes that evident (Zahavi 2001).

In their phenomenological account, Zahavi and Overgaard (2012), however, show that empathy is not the same as "social contagion" and affirm its role in interpersonal understanding. Howe aptly summarizes the difference between empathy and sympathy: "empathy puts me in your emotional shoes, sympathy simply tells you that I've walked there too" (2013, 12). Perhaps the best face-to-face situations involve the "I-Thou relation" that Martin Buber explicated; in these, "the individual enters into relation with the other with his or her whole and innermost being, in a meeting with real dialogue" (Lawrence-Lightfoot 1999). That means openness and willingness to enter in the other person's experience—as much as that is possible. Whatever the word used, that is the ideal. In such relationships the social construction of self is on the right track.

It has been said that most of us view other people as deficient versions of ourselves. Obviously this is far from an ethical approach; it is also antithetical to a phenomenological approach that focuses on true, authentic, fresh perceptions of the other person. As Levinas (1998, 75) asserts, "the other is in no way another myself, participating with me in a common existence. The relationship with the other is not an idyllic and harmonious relationship of communion, or a sympathy through which we put ourselves in the other's place; we recognize the other as resembling us, but exterior to us; the relationship with the other is a relationship with a Mystery."

We are awed at the presence of such a mystery; trying to understand this mystery means being open to the other person as a separate entity, focusing on him, acknowledging the "irreducible alterity of the other person" (Cohen 1987, 26). That means the other person is not I, deficient or perfect, but a separate person with her own intrinsic value. "This otherness and this absolute separation manifest themselves in the epiphany of the face, in the face to face" (Levinas 1998, 185). The person is before me now "as a neighbor" (1998, 9), not merely an object of my perception—not a phenomenon, not a complement to me, not an enemy, not a thing, an object, or a target of my actions, but as a subject in her own right. Ethical photographers, for example, ask permission before taking pictures of people, and later share these pictures with them.[3] Such thoughtfulness is constructive to the self-esteem of the people because it acknowledges them as unique subjects in their own right, and thus avoids objectification. As Levinas concludes, to understand the other "demands sympathy or love, ways of being that are different from impassive contemplation" (Levinas 1998, 5; cf. Schutz and Luckmann 1973, 64, quoted above).

In short, constructive interactions are those in which both parties feel affirmed in their separate selves. Ethics helps us examine the dimensions of supportive relationships that enhance the good for both. This is where teleological ethics, virtue ethics, and care ethics are together. Whether such affirming approach to others is sympathy or empathy, it means accepting the other as a mystery, a neighbor who is different from oneself. Yet one must have a healthy self-concept before one can really love and appreciate the other. Truly constructive interactions help develop such personhood in each partner.

CONCLUSION

This introductory chapter briefly examined some of the dynamics of the social construction and maintenance of self, a process in which our interactions with others play a definite role. While the Western worldview is predominantly centered on individual autonomy and responsibility for one's own conduct and even for one's own feelings, the effect that other people have on us—and conversely we have on them—is not to be ignored. With the help of phenomenology, this chapter explained the social construction of our self-concepts and showed how the fragile self is easily threatened in everyday interactions. To understand constructive interactions, several theories of ethics were reviewed, all of which emphasize the goal of enhancing human well-being by our behavior. Phenomenology helps us understand how we experience our interactions and how the experiences consequently affect our self-concepts, while ethics prescribes how we ought to behave toward other people in constructive ways.

The claim of this book is that an ethical approach toward other people is to recognize them as subjects who have a self, an agency, and their own goals in life; that is, to appreciate them as independent moral agents, and our task is to gear our behavior toward enhancing this capacity in others. To a certain extent, then, we are responsible for helping others around us become their best selves, thereby helping them reach their human potential. When such approach is reciprocal, a supportive community is created that enhances human thriving. To that end, the following chapters will focus more specifically on encounters, the problem of prejudice, and the ethics of respect.

NOTES

1. Turner disagrees with the prevalent sociological understanding of the inherent sociality of humans, attested to by many other scholars (e.g., Lieberman 2013). Since humans are apes, we are inherently individualistic, according to Turner, and have only later managed to overcome this tendency "to a degree," enough to develop social bonds (Turner 2002, 3, 58).

2. Dorothy Smith (1987, 66), however, convincingly argues that "Women have little opportunity for the exercise of mastery and control" of their own lives but "are generally means to the enterprises of others, or means to the enterprise built into an organizational process."

3. "When photographer Dawoud Bey talks about his art, he points to the 'development of a relationship' with his subjects as the center of his work" (Lawrence-Lightfoot 1999, 119). He asked for consent from the subjects before taking their pictures, and using a Polaroid camera he gave them a copy right away. Then after four years of working the streets, he had a 1979 show at the Studio Museum on 125th Street in Harlem. The exhibit, "Harlem USA" drew an audience of the very people he had photographed. For many of them, this was the first time they had been in a museum, and they were pleased to see themselves "on the wall" (Lawrence-Lightfoot 1999, 129–133).

Chapter Two

Interpersonal Encounters

While prejudicial attitudes toward groups of people affect social policy and other large-scale issues, individually held prejudices are evident in social interactions and have the ramifications on the self discussed in the previous chapter. Therefore understanding what goes on in social interactions is basic to understanding prejudice. All interpersonal association is made of separate encounters, so what goes on in such encounters carries a definite moral weight and has an effect on the self. The word "encounter" is used for various levels of social interaction, from between strangers to between acquaintances, friends, or intimates. For example, in the 1960s in the United States the word became known because of the "Encounter Group" movement and later the "Marriage Encounter" programs. Both of these were designed to help people communicate honestly and openly with one another—a different aim from that of casual encounters. This chapter will delve more deeply into some of the dynamics present in encounters, with an eye toward factors that make them positive. Whether our focus is on the initial meeting of two people or on repeated interactions, the fact is that when another human being comes face-to-face with us, two worlds confront one another and a most complicated event is at hand. Our attitudes and actions at that event may have far-reaching consequences.

Erving Goffman (1961, 1983) considers an encounter the most elemental unit of sociological analysis, and he defines a face-to-face encounter as interaction that involves "the reciprocal influence of individuals upon one another's actions when in one another's immediate physical presence" (1959, 15). The definition provides an appropriate basis for this chapter since my attention here too is on physical presence, not on distant encounters—such as via social media—that is an entirely different subject. My claim, however, is that the reciprocal influence in physical encounters is not only on actions but also on feelings, motivations, confidence, self-esteem, and other psychological dimensions of one or both parties. So much is involved in that instant that no study can account for every aspect. I am not specifically looking at the political viewpoints of the partners, neither the geographical location of the encounter or the time of day or season, though these too make a difference. My aim is to describe the most salient background factors and social and psychological dimensions that have bearing on the ethics of the encounter.

THE CONTEXT OF ENCOUNTERS

For the sake of simplicity, let us consider an encounter between two people, though some of the same dynamics and more are present when several people meet. When two people meet, there are two selves, with their unique personalities, emotions, perhaps different genders, ages, ethnicities, cultures, educational levels, types of upbringing and belief systems, goals, tastes, experiences, preferences, hang-ups, and relationships; all of these and more background factors may be different. We don't know what experiences the other person has had, what her needs and inclinations are, and what is going on in her life at the moment—whether she just had a fight with her spouse or boss, or even what she had for breakfast or lunch that day. And as Schutz (1967, 98–99) asserts (discussed in chapter 1), different people have different "stocks of knowledge," another fact that makes it impossible to fully understand the other person, to fully step in her shoes.

Similarly, one's own background is part of the context. We have what Husserl calls "perceptual sense," which refers to "the content of my sensory experience, including not just what directly meets my eye, but also a vast background of assumptions, memories, associations, and anticipation" (Carman 2012, ix). In other words, what we perceive has gone through a sift of our own previous experiences that help us make sense of the perceptual experience by filling in the missing parts, as Gestalt theory explains. This, however, is where prejudice plays a role, as the next chapter will show. Phenomenology calls us to "peel off" these culturally induced preconceptions and to be open to what is before us—as the phenomenologist Merleau-Ponty says, to "plunge into" the perception.

To these personal factors we have to add each party's embeddedness in the social structural and cultural context of the society or their different societies. Turner (2002, 30–41) divides social structure into three levels: the macro-level of institutions, the meso-level of corporate and categorical units (e.g., gender or race), and the micro-level of face-to-face interactions that is his and my focus. The macro- and meso-level realities are the larger structural entities in which we are embedded and within which interactions at the micro-level take place. The political and economic systems, other institutional structures and the culture of the society provide the larger context. For example, in Saudi Arabia women could not drive until recently, and even that under certain restrictions. Furthermore, until now they are required to have their heads covered when in public, though at present some brave women are challenging that rule. Looking for the larger good, that of women's liberation, they are willing to have negative encounters with the police—representatives of the institutional structure—and subject themselves to punishments, such as prison sentences and possible beatings.

Pertaining to the meso-level, the corporate and categorical units, each party in the interaction represents some corporate entity, perhaps an organization where he works, a spiritual center where he worships or some other social club in which he participates, at any rate a family context and a given social class and neighborhood, to name a few examples. The categories, such as gender, race, or age, are more visible than the corporate units, thus we tend to "place" individuals in their respective categorical units. This colors or guides the interaction and sometimes leads to mistaken assessments, such as undue trust (discussed in chapter 5), or belittling attitudes and behaviors, such as strangers calling a woman a "sweetie" or "baby" or a black man a "boy" or something worse. Actually, though these categories are at the meso-level, they are also personal characteristics that are experienced at the micro-level, therefore they color the interaction in warmer or colder hues. All our interactions are "nested" in the realities of these structural levels, as Turner (2002, 36–38) explains.

All levels of social structures are formed and operate in the context of culture that also guides our behavior at the micro-level. Our beliefs and values are largely dictated by our cultures, as are the norms, expectations, and practices in everyday life. Shared symbols enable us to understand one another (Mead 1934), and shared rituals, such as religious ceremonies or holiday customs, reinforce our cultural identities and produce solidarity (Durkheim 1912). As Goffman (1967) again explains, all interaction is governed by cultural rules that specify what behaviors are appropriate. The Maori people rub each other's noses when they greet each other, but in North America or Europe greeting a stranger that way would obviously not be acceptable. And though smiles are universal, the ever-present wide smiles of many Americans may seem strange to people from cultures that have more reserved interpersonal norms. One Afghan girl visiting the United States said: "In Afghanistan we laugh differently." And her friend added: "Yes, like, not loudly, and no teeth showing" (Harman 2019, A7).

For any interaction to occur, both participants must understand and share some symbols, and the universality of some symbols enables us to understand people from other cultures as well. As the philosopher Gadamer (1982) observes, on the basis of our shared humanity we have a common history and understanding, and these lead to "merging of horizons." Mark Twain's observation on his international travels, "I saw a mother smiling to her child," illustrates such cultural universals that make us one humanity. Human beings all over the globe have more commonalities than differences: "at least 99 percent of the DNA in all humans is *exactly* the same" (Christakis 2019, 408, emphasis his). When we see another human being we intuitively acknowledge our own kind, our own species being. Our common humanity places us "in the same boat" and thus makes interaction possible even with language barriers.

With this background, each participant's verbal and nonverbal behavior—words and the tone of voice, facial expressions, body postures, hand gestures, or other demeanor—create a communicative event that has consequences sometimes far beyond the encounter itself. In fact, the nonverbal behavior is often a better indicator of the person's real feelings than words are. Goffman describes a Shetland Isle hostess happily observing her guest's gusto with which he consumes the meal while accepting his verbal compliments with a polite smile (1959, 7). Most likely the gusto makes her happier than the compliments do and will inspire her for future cooking. This implies that behavioral clues give a truer message of real feelings than polite words do.

The point here about culture is that we internalize such norms and symbols, so that our "normal" behavior follows these cultural rules. They simplify our lives by providing us with automatic responses so that we don't need to deliberate what to do in each situation, and most of the time we blindly follow them. But as Habermas (1987) explains, modern society has lead to an "internal colonization" of the lifeworld—the world we experience—by the system; in other words, the system with its institutional and cultural rules begins to control the subjective world of the individual. All systems exercise some control; the degree depends mainly on the type of the political institution. Mostly, the system is a guide but need not be the master of our interactions. We can question or even challenge the cultural norms, as some women in Saudi Arabia are doing, and in this the system and their lifeworlds interact.

The discussion above identifies some of the multitude of contextual factors present in an interpersonal encounter. Both parties have their unique personality characteristics, backgrounds, and intentions, as well as internalized cultural symbols and institutional norms. Thus none of us has a "God's eye" view of the world or of other people; we always see from somewhere (Merleau-Ponty 2012; Dorothy Smith 1987), resulting in a partial and imperfect view. These factors and more—such as the characteristics of the situation—influence all our encounters. It is only because both participants are human beings and therefore have "merged horizons" (Gadamer 1982) that there can be any interaction at all.[1] Belonging to the same human family makes interaction possible even with language barriers, yet understanding these human limitations helps us place the interaction in context and refrain from passing a negative judgment on the other person's behavior.

INTERPERSONAL PERCEPTION

Examining what happens when another human being enters in our field of vision takes us first to the phenomenology of perception. But we shall focus only on factors present in interpersonal perception, not on the entire theory that is beyond the purpose of this book. The initial perception of a human being usually does not differ greatly from object perception. As Merleau-Ponty (2012, 363) writes, "in some respect, each object will at first be a natural object; if it is to be able to enter into my life, it must be made of colors and of tactile and sonorous qualities." Walking on a road, I see a vertical object in the distance. I can see it is neither a tree nor a scarecrow; it is on the road and is moving toward me. Because I have seen people before, especially on this road, my previous experience helps me through the cognitive process to identify the object as a human being (Treisman and Gelade 1980). But only when this now identified member of my own species gets close enough to enable communication will she or he cease being an object, and the event now becomes an interpersonal encounter.

Like objects, people are part of the "ecological affordances" the environment offers us (Gibson 1979), and we all are part of that ecology. We are not really separate entities but part of a Gestalt, immersed in the world of things and other people, part of the total scene. Thus "we must no longer conceive of perception as a constitution of the real object, but rather as our inherence in things" (Merleau-Ponty 2012, 366). Now a piece of that world, however, is confronting me in the form of another human being who is like me and yet not like me. He has his different personality characteristics and his unique background, and he represents a cultural world that is more ambiguous than the natural world and therefore brings more complications to the perceptual event and more work for the cognitive process. Reflecting on this phenomenon, Merleau-Ponty states (2012, 364): "the analysis of the perception of others encounters the essential difficulty raised by the cultural world because it must resolve the paradox of a consciousness seen from the outside, the paradox of a thought that resides in the exterior and that, when compared to my own, is already without a subject and is anonymous."

Seeing an object is straightforward and easy because we can stop at the exterior, but now that is not sufficient. As Merleau-Ponty asks, "If my consciousness has a body, why would other bodies not 'have' consciousness?" Now the most important aspect of the body before me is what is inside; there is another interior to which I have no access. Yet this other consciousness is equally part of the world in which we both are immersed. How can I comprehend this consciousness, a fellow human being yet different from me, another "I"? Fortunately, there are clues. What matters is not the bodily mass of flesh and blood but "the behaviors that take shape upon these visible bodies." A "perceptual consciousness" is "the subject of a behavior" and has "that expressive instrument that we call a face" (Merleau-Ponty 2012, 367). Thus the consciousness becomes visible and available for my perception, though I must admit that it still remains a mystery.

Our perception of another person begins with a glance, and as Schroeder observes, there is more to it "than meets the eye." It is an acknowledgment of the other person, "the first phenomenal occurrence of the face-to-face encounter." There is power to this "listening eye" that can at least influence if not persuade the other (Schroeder 2006, 99, 101). The rich communication present in a mere glance colors if not defines the subsequent stages of the interaction, and can sometimes steer the day of the participant(s) in a positive or negative direction. Personally, I have experienced brief, unexpected encounters that have made a big difference in my day. Once in my graduate school days I wanted to see a certain professor in the psychology department on a Friday afternoon, only to be disappointed that his office was closed. My face must have expressed frustration because a young man—I assumed another graduate student—greeted me with such soothing demeanor that my frustration dissipated then and there. Calmly I realized that Monday is coming and with that another opportunity to see the professor. I had no idea who the young man was, neither did he know anything about me, but with a glance he read the visual symbols of frustration on my face and responded in a manner that put me at ease.

A glance also occurs in a social structural and cultural context, and sometimes is accompanied by far more menacing implications than in my benign example above. In his book *Between the World and Me*, Ta-Nehisi Coates describes the fear he grew up with in his Baltimore neighborhood. One incident, when he was just eleven years old, stays in his mind. Standing among a group of boys in front of a 7-Eleven store, admiring the kids' sense of fashion, he "focused in on a light-skinned boy with a long head and small eyes" who was "scowling at another boy" close to Ta-Nehisi. "The boy with the small eyes reached into his ski jacket and pulled out a gun . . . and in his small eyes I saw a surging rage that could, in an instant, erase my body." He did not shoot, thanks to other boys pulling him back, but he "had affirmed my place in the order of things." Coates contrasts this situation with "other worlds where children did not regularly fear for their bodies," worlds "organized around pot roasts, blueberry pies, fireworks, ice-cream sundaes, immaculate bathrooms, and small toy trucks that were loosed in wooded backyards with streams and glens" (Coates 2015, 19–20).

In any case, with a glance we can read the other's emotions as well as express our own. Often an unexpected sunny smile has warmed up my world.

But a smile can give quite a different message at different times, depending on the type of smile, the situation, the frame of mind of each of the parties, and the prior relationship between the parties. For example, there is a difference between a happy or friendly smile and a smirk. Turner considers emotions "one of the most critical forces driving face-to-face interaction," something that is central in Freud's theory and is also present in Cooley's sociological theory (both discussed in chapter 1). Turner identifies four types of primary emotions: assertion-anger, aversion-fear, satisfaction-happiness, and disappointment-sadness (2002, 67–68). When someone cuts in front of you in traffic you are most likely to experience assertion-anger and may honk the horn, and when a white person crosses the street at the approach of someone representing a racial minority, she is unduly exhibiting aversion-fear. Coates's example above showed both anger and fear, respectively. But when we meet a friend our face shows our satisfaction-happiness, and I must have exhibited the disappointment-sadness emotion at the professor's door. Thus emotions can be read from nonverbal gestures and expressions, and they bind us together as human beings and can inspire or inhibit personal aspirations.

In his functionalist theory of society, the sociologist Talcott Parsons also includes emotion in his analysis of social action. He identifies the three elementary components of a system of action as cognition, cathexis, and evaluation. According to him, cognition always involves cathexis, the investment of emotional significance. Parsons explains this cathectic orientation as "the significance of ego's relation to the object or objects in question for the gratification-deprivation balance of his personality" (1951, 7). While such object-perception implies focus on the self, in interpersonal situations the glance means perceiving another subject, and the cathectic emotional involvement means that we infuse value to the encounter. Cathexis works with the cognitive process that orients our attention to "the relevant aspects of the situation in their relevance to the actor's interests" (Parsons 1951, 7). This means that perception is selective, geared to what confirms one's self (Turner 2002, 8). For Goffman, a major interest would be the desire to present oneself in a positive light. I doubt that was the motivation of the young man who calmed me down; he may have wished to practice his budding profession as a psychologist, or simply to comfort a person in apparent distress. The youngster with a gun in Baltimore, on the other hand, wanted to show his power. The ethical challenge in interpersonal perception is to take into account the other person's interests, not just one's own, as the young man in the psychology department did.

As Parsons asserts, both cognition and cathexis are present in any unit of interpersonal action. Thus an emotional dimension is always present, whether the situation is pleasant, unpleasant, or apparently neutral. It directs our attention to the issue or item that is of interest to us, and the initial glance communicates the type of emotion present. As there are many different possibilities of orientation, the selection is made through evaluation, the third basic category in Parson's action theory. In the above quotation from Parsons, he discusses "ego's relation to the object or objects." It is through evaluation that we determine our relation to the object of our perception and decide on the course of the unfolding interaction.

The idea of typification, explained in the previous chapter, suggests a rational classification of our perceptions into one or another of the meso-level structures discussed above. Now we see a person and our natural attitude with its typification schemes classifies the person as a man or a woman, representative of a certain race or occupational group—for example a construction worker or a professional going to her office. But as Levinas and others assert, beyond such surface level typifications (which could be wrong) the other is a mystery to us, radically Other. There is much more to a person than an objective category. Furthermore, unlike the perception of objects, person perception—including it's accompanying typifications—is reciprocal: in a face-to-face encounter we are "checking each other out" (Kenny 1994, 1) and assigning each other into categories. Though we share the same "vivid present" (Berger and Luckmann 1967, 28), each of us experiences the encounter differently from the other, thus the effect on each of us is different. Even when the two participants know each other or have some previous shared history, understanding one another's intentions is not automatic.

Whereas a glance is a necessary beginning of a perception, a gaze is something different, almost akin to a stare. Gaze may involve admiration or wonder—such as in stargazing, but a stare implies surprise at seeing something unusual, an expression that polite people try to prevent or at least hide. Parents would admonish their toddler not to stare at a differentially abled person, for example. Whether we gaze or stare at someone, it may make that person feel uncomfortable because it makes her an object.[2] It may make the person feel that she is under evaluation, and that is objectification even when the evaluation is positive. This has implications also for the person who is doing the gazing or staring: he is standing at the sidelines, not participating in life with the other, not joining with the neighbor. Merleau-Ponty (2012, 378) writes that such "inhuman gaze" objectifies the other in a harmful way "because it takes the place of possible communication." Furthermore, if I participate and he is sitting on the side watching me, I may feel that I am being evaluated; he is a spectator and I am an object of his observation. When we both participate we share the same experiences, the same reality. Participation helps a person belong and creates community with the other participants.

To further complicate matters, our initial perceptions may be illusionary. Your stock of knowledge may lead you to define a modest-looking old woman as uneducated, but you observe her checking out a philosophy book at the library and thus correct your stereotypical perception by a true, genuine perception of her as an intellectual—especially if you hear her conversing about the book. One must be open to such corrections or verifications that repeated perceptions provide (Merleau-Ponty 2012, 308–11). Similarly, to define people by the color of their skin is to see them only externally, as inanimate objects; or to infer from external features supposed behaviors is to guess, based on stereotypes. It may be a totally false perception or at least an incomplete one. Merleau-Ponty (2012, 70) explains that to really focus on something I "anchor myself in it" or "plunge into it." This involves intentional centering on the object, and in case of human beings it must mean looking beyond (or beneath) physical appearance.

The custom of greeting a person is a sign of acknowledging him as a human being. That is the basic, fundamental level; it communicates a message that we are dealing with a person and not a thing. Even in a group meeting, when we take time to introduce ourselves to each other we acknowledge each other's humanness, that the bodies present are persons and not a field of cabbage. But in chance encounters, it is through evaluation that we decide what kind of greeting is appropriate, or if there is need for any greeting. There is a difference in the United States between rural acknowledgment of others and those in cities where crowds are the norm. In rural Kansas motorists raise their hand in greeting one another on country roads, but that would be unthinkable on highways or in New York City. And in Carmel, California, residents compliment each other's dogs on the sidewalk. By that they not only acknowledge their admiration of the other dog but also reveal their love for dogs.

Manners of greeting, of course, are dictated by cultural norms: in some cultures they are more elaborate than in others, like the rubbing of noses mentioned above or kisses on both cheeks. At any rate, ignoring a person omits an acknowledgment of her humanness—a necessary omission in crowds, though even then people generally avoid bumping into each other. But when they do bump, an apology is a kind of greeting. Coates (2015, 119) describes how he accidentally bumped into another black man and said "My bad," to which the other responded "You straight," the spontaneous exchange showing their "private rapport." An encounter takes place, however, whether the participants greet each other or not. "In every attitude toward a human being there is a greeting—even if it is the refusal of a greeting" (Levinas 1998, 7). Further evaluation, influenced by cultural norms, then determines the type of relationship or situation and thus our subsequent action-orientation; for example, avoidance, exchanging a friendly greeting and a quick comment with the dog-walker, a more involved encounter with an acquaintance, or stopping to help someone in distress.

To summarize thus far, interpersonal perception is rich in nuances. Though initially any perception identifies an object, the difference is quickly evident: what we perceive now is another subject with his own culture, personality, and other background factors. The perception begins with a glance, but it involves emotional engagement and an evaluation that may make us correct our initial perception. Although the other person is different from ourselves—totally Other, he belongs to the same human family. Thus we have shared universal norms and symbols and a shared identity in spite of differences.

DEFINITION OF THE SITUATION

Looking at an interpersonal encounter through another sociological lens, each encounter requires an instantaneous "definition of the situation." In the words of W. I. Thomas (1923) who coined the phrase, this is "a stage of examination and deliberation" that is "preliminary to any self-determined act of behavior." Obviously, the context makes a big difference on how the situation is defined. This includes the above-described elements of both personal backgrounds of the participants and those of social structure and culture.

Racial profiling is an example of a negative definition based on the race of the other. Perhaps in no other situation is there a need for such speed in the "examination and deliberation" than in encounters between the police and some minority citizens in the United States of America where faulty perceptions have too often resulted in undue arrest or more serious violence. I know of one instance in which an African American man was arrested, accused of theft, while carrying his wife's fur coat to a dry cleaner. And Professor Henry Louis Gates, Jr. was arrested getting into his own house, accused of a break-in (Goodnough 2009). But even more serious consequences often result from racial definitions of situations. Coates discusses several instances in which a police officer has killed an innocent black child or young man. One victim was Prince Jones, an ardent Christian young man, "patron saint of the twice as good," son of highly educated parents, who was chased from Maryland through Washington, D.C. to Virginia and killed for no reason (Coates 2015, 77–88). This is just one of many such tragic incidents, reported in the news and then forgotten. Coates concludes: the safety of "those who lived in the Dream" was "in schools, portfolios, and skyscrapers. Ours was in men with guns who could only view us with the same contempt as the society that sent them" (2015, 85).

From the viewpoint of a young black male, an encounter with a police officer often means danger because of racial profiling and past violent encounters between the police and innocent black males. This may lead to efforts to run away or other means of avoidance of the encounter, or to standing one's ground because attempting to escape may indicate guilt. From the viewpoint of a police officer, there is danger because of the possibility of the person having a gun, even when none is displayed—at least that is the often-presented excuse. The cultural and institutional backgrounds play a role here: when the society allows individuals to carry guns, the police immediately think of the possibility of their presence and use and therefore are more ready to resort to violence. Thus both sides are often led to define the situation as danger. This is one example of the system influencing encounters, and it illustrates the importance of the glance and a quick definition of the situation with speedy evaluation.

Encounters with the police also illustrate the two sides of any definition of an interpersonal situation. Seeing another body with its behavior, we can only make sense of it "through analogy of my own behavior and my own inner experience, which teaches me the sense and the intension of the perceived gestures" (Merleau-Ponty 2012, 364), like the police observing the suspect putting his hand in his pocket and assuming he is reaching for a gun. And as Gibson (1979) observes in the context of his ecological theory of perception, the other's behavior "affords" or brings about one's own behavior. Misinterpreting the other's behavior may unintentionally bring about negative responses.

Another dimension in the definition of a social situation is impression management. Goffman (1959) emphasizes the manipulative nature of our behaviors toward other people, our efforts to put ourselves in positive light. But not all behavior is manipulative. Features of the situation make a difference—a job interview is certainly different from a casual encounter, and much depends on one's personality characteristics. A narcissistic personality is more apt to manipulation, and examples of it abound. But that is different from appropriate self-confidence and assertiveness that operates on a level playing field and does not use the other person for one's own ends. Furthermore, different statuses and roles and degrees of social power of the participants bring different expectations to the encounter; if these are similar, the script for the interaction is clearer from the beginning, but if some or all of these factors differ substantively, there is a gulf to overcome before mutual understanding can be achieved.

Let us imagine a very benign type of everyday, impersonal encounter that illustrates how in one situation different contexts and definitions of the situation come together: meeting with a cashier behind the counter in a grocery store. We define the situation as a business transaction, taking place within the economic system of our country, and we act accordingly. Objectively, the person behind the counter simply helps us pay for our shopping. But he is a person and thus preferable to a machine; many—including myself—still prefer this live helper to the option of paying at an automated lane. Unlike the chat you may have with a friend you run into, you merely greet this person and may exchange a few words. You are in a hurry to get home to make dinner, and from the cashier's viewpoint you may be the 150th person that he is encountering during his shift and his feet are hurting. In Goffman's words, there is a "working consensus" in that you both define the situation similarly as a brief economic encounter and are eager for its swift execution. It is not a social visit, especially if there is a long line behind you. Your different social realities (Schutz and Luckmann 1973) are not relevant in this transaction, but you acknowledge each other's humanity by exchanging a greeting.

In all perception we automatically act out the "Thomas Theorem" (Thomas and Thomas 1928, 572): if people "define situations as real, they are real in their consequences." The above-mentioned situations of perceived danger for both parties in police encounters have become real and sometimes resulted in drastic consequences. Once I was driving to a conference with a male Japanese professor beside me in the passenger seat. Lost in South Chicago, we noticed a white woman walking on the sidewalk and stopped, opening the car window, to ask for directions. Without responding, the woman quickly ran away. For whatever reason, she obviously defined the situation as a real danger and acted accordingly.

Definitions of situations, while depending on circumstances and personal characteristics of the participants, are culturally shaped and occur almost automatically; and the situations are always in situ, place-bound, adding other dynamics. The above-mentioned woman probably as a rule did not talk to strangers in South Chicago. Furthermore, stereotypes take hold early in the interaction; research has shown that Euro-Americans high in implicit prejudice perceive threatening affect more on black than white faces (Hugenberg and Bodenhausen 2003). Situational factors like the time of day—daytime or night—also make a difference. Obviously, any "projected definition of the situation also has a distinctive moral character" (Goffman 1959, 13), especially when we think of the consequences. When a person's overwhelming feeling is fear in most interpersonal encounters out in the world, negative dynamics are created that too easily bring about negative consequences.

As mentioned briefly earlier, Coates's description of growing up in Baltimore's black neighborhoods meant experiencing fear on many fronts. "It was always right in front of me"—in being "naked before the elements of the world, before all the guns, fists, knives, crack, rape, and disease"; in the boys dressed "in their armor against their world"; in his own father who loved him, yet at times resorted to "his black leather belt" (2015, 14–15, 17); and in school:

> I came to see the streets and the schools as arms of the same beast. One enjoyed the official power of the state while the other enjoyed its implicit sanction. But fear and violence were the weaponry of both. Fail in the streets and the crews would catch you slipping and take your body. Fail in the schools and you would be suspended and sent back to those same streets, where they would take your body. And I began to see these two arms in relation—those who failed in the schools justified their destruction in the streets. The society

could say, "He should have stayed in school," and then wash its hands of him. (Coates 2015, 33)

Systemic reform is obviously needed to remedy this situation of wide-ranging fear that a large section of the population is experiencing, with far-reaching consequences.

Special challenges are present in encounters between volunteers and clients in welfare work. For most people, asking for material help, whether food, clothing, or money, is demeaning. In a success-oriented society it is an admission of failure, so the definition of the situation is that of humiliation. Such was the case for Alene, a Philippine immigrant I talked with in a church-operated food pantry in 2014. She was educated and a brave, hard-working woman; it was difficult for her to accept that she needed help. She had to quit her job because of health reasons, yet must provide for an elderly mother and five children. Necessity made her accept the humiliation of coming to the food bank. Some others may not feel as humiliated or—perhaps attempting to hide their humiliation—may act in an aggressive or demanding way. The volunteers, pressed by hard work, may not always consider how the clients feel about the situation. This may lead to treating them as numbers in a line of needy people and not as unique persons with unique circumstances.

In an earlier research (Terian 1984), interview respondents (volunteers in various church charities) often emphasized the difference between the treatment of clients in government welfare agencies and church programs. According to them, welfare agencies deal with their clients in a cold manner as numbers, whereas in church programs they do it with love and respect. This assessment, of course, reflected the idealistic goal of the religious helpers more than the reality in many cases. Many emphasized the effort to get to know the recipients of help by personal encounters, even in their homes, whereas others preferred to extend their assistance indirectly through social service agencies. Even the "loving" personal encounters in a "charity" situation, however, may be humiliating to the recipient, as apparently most of the volunteers felt as they themselves would need to be in a very dire need—just about destitute—before they would ask for help.[3] The definition of the situation is different for the helper from that of the client, and even for the latter it depends on cultural norms, the degree of need, and many other factors.

Many of the volunteers in the research described being embarrassed when the client was extremely grateful. Such an encounter apparently drove home to them the injustice involved in the situation, that the recipient was forced to submit to such a humiliating experience. But even those who don't show gratitude or who appear aloof may be reacting to the humiliation of the situation, as Shirley in a Catholic Church's welfare program speculated (Terian 1984, 286). And some Presbyterian deacons described being surprised when people refused to accept a Thanksgiving basket, yet acknowledged that it would be hard for themselves to accept it were they in that situation. When someone is at the door with a basket of food, the definition of the situation depends on how dire the need is, among other things. Yet many felt that personal contact is better than "distant charity" that easily leads to stereotyping (Terian 1984, 309, 333).

But personal contact doesn't always help us define the situation correctly. In a recent book, *Talking to Strangers*, Malcolm Gladwell (2019) describes instances in which a definition of the situation has gone seriously wrong in spite of or because of personal contact. One case study is about a police encounter in which Sandra Bland was unduly arrested, later leading to her death. Another describes British Prime Minister Neville Chamberlain's apparently blind trust in Adolph Hitler after he had met him three times in 1938. Chamberlain thought that he had averted war, but soon the Second World War and Holocaust started, in spite of Hitler's signed agreement to hold off his ambitions. Yet another case study is about the fraudulent financial organization of Bernard Madoff to whose Ponzi scheme many people entrusted their money, only to lose it all. The multiple case studies Gladwell analyzes show our inability to accurately assess a stranger's trustworthiness. "We think we can easily see into the hearts of others based on the flimsiest of clues," Gladwell states and concludes, "We have a *default to truth*" (Gladwell 2019, 50, 73, emphasis his). This is an important dimension of interpersonal encounters: caution need not mean disrespect, and ethical encounters need not mean blind trust in strangers. Keeping respectful distance is not unethical; there is a difference between a proven trusted friend and a stranger, however charming his ways may be (more of this in the last chapter).

The above examples illustrate the quick definitions of the situations that take place daily in our interpersonal encounters. The macro-level cultural and institutional backgrounds as well as the meso-level categorizations influence actions at the micro-level of interpersonal behavior. As discussed in chapter 1, ethical behavior calls for attention and care to act with the other person's best in mind: rather than acting spontaneously with our "id," acting with our superego (to use Freud's idioms), not manipulating the situations solely to our own advantage, neither allowing others to take advantage of us. Our prejudices—to be discussed in the next chapter—take hold of our automatic responses. Before closing this chapter, however, we must glance at interactions that form and maintain long-term relationships. Even in such relationships, interpersonal association is made of encounters that involve ongoing definitions of situations, and these become building blocks of the relationship.

ENCOUNTERS IN CLOSER RELATIONSHIPS

The discussion above focused mainly on fleeting encounters between strangers. But relationships are built of repeated encounters, and in that case the moral weight of the encounters is heavier. Friendships are built of positive encounters that ideally would extend to home life as well. But while societal norms usually lead a person to be polite to strangers, at home the guard is often off and feelings are freely expressed. This may lead to verbal conflicts, hurt feelings, tears, domestic violence, and other struggles common in intimate relationships. As the Encounter Group Movement has acknowledged, encounters are fraught with problems in close relationships, yet one should feel safe to be oneself, and that should be reciprocal.

Different definitions of the situation definitely affect relationships between spouses. Think of busy parents coming from work, picking up their children from day care or an after-school program. Each member of the family has had different experiences that color their moods and expectations of the evening at home. There is dinner to prepare and clean up, children's homework to supervise, perhaps a load or two of laundry, worry about the next day at work, and so on. Maybe the rule is that the spouse who comes home first will start the dinner. One wife said proudly that if she has onion and garlic in the frying pan when her husband comes home, the appetizing smell makes him happy to know that dinner is coming. In that case the definition of the situation is positive and all is well. Better yet, he may join his wife in preparing the dinner, acknowledging that she is busy too and grasping the opportunity for some time together. Some other husband might define the situation differently and yell at the wife for not having the dinner ready. Perceptions of an identical situation may differ because of numerous other factors, such as each spouse's day at work, their personalities, the marital relationship, and so on. During his first campaign for president, Barak Obama described an incident from his days at the Senate. On his way home to Chicago for the weekend, his mind was full of thoughts about the weighty deliberations on the Senate floor when Michelle called and asked him to stop on the way and buy an ant trap. "An ant trap!" he exclaimed, waking up to a different reality. "Yes," she insisted, "we have ants." All families must tackle the task of uniting such diverse worlds when they come together at night.

Every marriage involves some tensions and disagreements, as the Swiss-born British philosopher Alain deBotton (2016) explains in a very insightful opinion article in *The New York Times,* entitled "Why You Marry the Wrong Person." Criticizing the overly romanticized idea of modern marriage, he writes: "every human will frustrate, anger, annoy, madden and disappoint us—and we will (without any malice) do the same to them." There is no other person "who shares our every taste," so the key to a successful relationship is to "negotiate differences in taste intelligently," tolerate them "with generosity," and employ a "more forgiving, humorous, and kindly perspective" toward our partner. My only criticism of this realistic and very wise article is that it assumes equality between the spouses; in many cases there is an unequal power relationship that precludes negotiations in good faith, a situation that brings additional challenges to a long-term relationship and in some cases necessitates a separation.

The point here is that a long-term relationship is made of separate encounters, and the nature of these encounters with their cumulative effect defines the relationship and even shapes each partner. It is a well-established fact that spouses who have been married for decades often begin to resemble each other and even "finish one another's sentences." Aside from that, as discussed in chapter 1, ongoing affirming feedback helps a person become an emotionally healthy, well-adjusted individual, and the need for recognition exists throughout one's life. Yet realistically we must acknowledge that negative interactions are part of life, so what is the answer? In the Family Formation Project at the University of Washington in Seattle ("Love Lab"), researchers have found that simply being nice to each other most of the time is key to a long-term relationship. As Gottman, director of the lab, summarizes it, satisfied couples maintained a five-to-one ratio of positive to negative moments in their relationship, but those heading for divorce had the ratio slip to below one-to-one (Gottman 1994; Benson 2017).

How can we create and sustain such mutually respectful and satisfying encounters? The phenomenology of perception includes this dimension as well. In one of his radio lectures in 1948, Merleau-Ponty (2004, 88) states: "We are continually obliged to work on our differences, to explain things we have said that have not been properly understood, to reveal what is hidden within us and to perceive other people." This, of course, requires patience and willingness to listen and consider the other's viewpoint as at least a viable alternative to ours. Criticizing Merleau-Ponty's earlier discussion of the body and its projection as dominating, Shannon Sullivan offers the idea of hypothetical construction. This method means that one would offer one's ideas to the other merely as hypotheses, to be worked on together. Such a process "must take these subjects' differences into account," and in making dialogue explicit it can "prevent the assumption of the familiar in another and thus the narrow reading and misunderstanding of her" (Sullivan 1997, 8, 13). If both participants approach the interaction with such honest, respectful, and humble attitude, a mutually supportive relationship is created, and that is the basis for a positive community, friendship, or marriage.

Encounters consisting of negotiation are respectful, and they require care. In other words, understanding—and thus smoothing our differences—needs constant attention in our interactions. Even when the two participants know each other or have some previous shared history, understanding one another's intentions is not automatic. It requires respect (the subject of chapter 4), listening, accepting the other as a mystery, not assuming one knows what the other thinks, and being open to differing viewpoints. Disagreements can also be respectful; they imply that one has considered the other person's viewpoint. With respectful disagreements the participants can still affirm one another as capable and valuable human beings—and more than that, as friends. Very wisely, deBotton (2016) concludes that in marriage "compatibility is an achievement of love; it must not be its precondition."[4]

CONCLUSION

Since people in interpersonal encounters bring with them their own worlds with a multitude of background, contextual, and personal factors, an encounter is an extremely complicated event. No one study can do justice to all its dimensions. In this chapter I have tried to explain the effect of encounters not only on the participants' actions but also on their feelings, emotions, and motivations. Because encounters show various degrees of respect or lack of it, they have an ethical dimension. The social context of encounters includes macro-, meso-, and micro-levels. At the macro-level are culture with its symbols and norms and institutional structures, at the meso-level corporate and categorical entities in which both participants are embedded, and at the micro-level each person's backgrounds and characteristics. All these different contextual factors influence our perceptions and behaviors and make interactions challenging.

An encounter begins with a perception of an object that in this case quickly must be acknowledged as another consciousness and thus different from us, though we both are embedded in the world and therefore are part of the same Gestalt. With a mere glance one can often read the feelings and emotions of the other—though not always their trustworthiness, and with a greeting we acknowledge that other's humanness. Shared symbols and common humanity make interaction possible even with language barriers. Yet care must be taken to avoid objectification because it denies the other's humanness.

Definitions of the situation of the encounter are culturally shaped and depend on contextual factors, and they bring about consequences. We act according to our own definitions, yet the other person most likely has a different definition. We react to the clues we read on the other's face, as that person responds to ours. The ethical challenge is to perceive the situation also from the other person's viewpoint, at least to acknowledge the difference and thus be open to a correction of our perception. If both partners have an open, hypothetical attitude, encounters can be positive and affirming to both. Lasting relationships depend on negotiating the differences and making sure that most communications are positive and affirming.

Whether as fleeting chance meetings or as moments in ongoing relationships, encounters are tangible events in which the self is either threatened and weakened or supported and strengthened. Ethical encounters are ones that enhance each party's sense of self and motivate them toward the realization of their potentials and dreams. As the next chapter shows, prejudice—a preconceived idea—is present in all perceptions and thus colors the interaction in lighter or darker hues with their different consequences.

NOTES

1. This does not rule out interactions with animals. When I take a walk and pass someone coming from the opposite direction with a dog, very often the dog is eager to interact with me. Yet human interactions—even with no shared language—have a different nature.

2. The case of a model may be an exception, but that role is by choice, and both the model and the spectators participate in one event, each playing their roles. Objectification, however, is part of the job, as one model noted: "Every day that you're working as a model, you're objectified somehow" (*New York Times* online briefing, 7 September 2017).

3. Similarly, the Jewish prayer book instructs worshippers to pray to God to "not make us need others' gifts or loans" (cited in Nadler and Jeffrey 1986, 82).

4. In my MA thesis (Terian 1981) I developed a theoretical framework of interpersonal relationships, from strangers and acquaintances to friends and intimates.

Chapter Three

Prejudice

By showing the social nature of self and the dimensions of encounters that have an effect on one's faith in oneself, the two previous chapters attempted to provide a context and establish the importance of the concept of prejudice, the subject of this chapter. This concept is getting considerable attention, justifiably so; we hear frequently about it especially in the context of race relations, and we are rightly admonished to do our best to eliminate its negative manifestations. But the term is generally understood in its narrow, simplistic meaning as something to be strictly avoided, without consideration of the impossibility and even undesirability of the demand if we look at the larger picture with the different dimensions of the concept. After all, prejudice not only colors our approach toward other people and groups but also is basic in our perception of most everything. This chapter first examines the meaning of the concept of prejudice and how it is related to stereotypes. A look at the historical development of the concept will then show that it was not always viewed negatively, and will describe factors that led to its negative definition. This is followed by focus on some of the effects of prejudice on the person at the receiving end, and that will lead us to the concept of positive prejudice—the ideal and ethical attitude toward other people. The chapter ends with an examination of the ideas of toleration and recognition, and their relation to prejudice.

WHAT IS PREJUDICE?

Prejudice is defined as an attitude toward people on the basis of their membership in a group (e.g., Jones 2002, 4; Brown 2010, 7; Dovidio et al. 2010, 5), usually a group that has particular, identifiable characteristics. This attitude is based on generalizing from what we know or think we know about the group or some of its members; that is the cognitive component. The affective or emotional component is how we feel about these people based on what we think we know. This affective component could logically be either positive— usually about one's ingroup—or negative, generally about an "other" or an outgroup that is different in some characteristics. Most recent discussions on prejudice acknowledge the possibility of a positive meaning but quickly settle on the negative because that is where prejudice becomes a social prob- lem (e.g., Allport 1954; Sampson 1999; Jones 2002; Stangor 2009; Brown 2010; Dovidio et al. 2010). My claim is, however, that to fully understand the nature of prejudice we need to examine it in its deeper, larger sense as the orientation that directs our attention and subsequent actions.

That leads us to another distinction between different types of prejudice, one that focuses on the degree of awareness of one's prejudice. Explicit prejudice is "intentional, controllable, and consciously held," whereas im- plicit prejudice is "positive or negative associations with a target group that are largely—though potentially not entirely" beneath awareness (Chen and Ratliff 2018, 302). In experimental research, Hahn and his associates found that the "participants were surprisingly accurate in their predictions" of their own implicit biases, as measured by the well-known Implicit Association Test (IAT).[1] But they note that the "participants tended to label their biases as 'weak,'" (in possible comparison with others, though that was not meas- ured), which suggests only "limited awareness of the scope and severity of their biases." Furthermore, the authors acknowledge that being asked in the research brought the participants' biases to their attention; the research does not inform us whether the participants would be aware of their biases if not asked (Hahn et al. 2014, 1369, 1389). The research thus shows that aware- ness of one's implicit bias or prejudice is partial at best.

The explicit type of prejudice or bias leads to explicit responses—such as overt, intentional discrimination, whereas the implicit orientations involve attitudes like stereotyping and can lead to "unintentional activation" (Dovi- dio et al. 2010, 10). Overt prejudice and discrimination are no longer wide- spread in the Western world, and most people would deny being racists, but implicit examples of negative prejudice are something that marginalized groups experience daily. These are often subconscious words, expressions or behaviors directed toward a member of an outgroup that intend no harm but show underlying insensitivity to the feelings of the Other by making him feel as an "Other." In 1970, a psychiatrist and Harvard University Professor, Chester M. Pierce, coined the term "microaggressions" to describe such ex- periences of African Americans. The term is in widespread use today and is applied to similar experiences of other marginalized groups, such as women, sexual minorities, and members of lower classes.

Professor Derald Wing Sue, who has written two books on microaggres- sions (2010a, 2010b), defines them as "brief, everyday exchanges that send denigrating messages to certain individuals because of their group membership," and he separates these from just any insults that any person may experience; that is, microaggressions are unintentional and unconscious insults—or to put it more mildly, putdowns—addressed to a member of a marginalized group. There are multiple examples, an abundance given by Sue and many given in this book in other contexts, such as a white woman crossing the street at the approach of a black man, or a white person not sitting beside a black person on a subway, or a woman being interrupted in a meeting (sometimes her idea being given by a man later and then enthusiastically accepted), or sexual objectification (Nadal 2014). Even "the simple act of asking someone their ethnicity, without any conversation prompting it, feels like drawing a figurative line in the sand. . . . The need to self-identify feels like having to validate myself to total strangers" (Ocampo 2019).

In a PBS Newshour interview, Professor Sue described these microaggressions that can "come out in ways that are outside the level of conscious awareness of an individual." He further commented: "our studies do indicate that it's the hidden, unintentional forms of bias that are most damaging to people of color" because they are "hard to prove, hard to quantify in some way, and very difficult for us to take action against because people oftentimes don't perceive it as harmful and significant" (Sue 2015). He gave an example of being constantly asked where he was born, and people not believing that he was born in the United States. This may make the person feel like a "perpetual alien or foreigner" in one's own country (Sue's words). Similarly, an immigrant with a foreign accent is sometimes told: "your accent defines who you are." Most likely the person making the statement intends no harm, but to the recipient of the statement it reinforces her foreign status, her otherness. There is a certain built-in reserve toward an Other that easily slips in even well-meaning communications, and to be at the receiving end of such communications for most if not all of one's life is stressful and harmful to one's self-esteem.

Implicit biases and their accompanying stereotypical thinking are of particular interest in the discussion here because of their largely unintentional nature that colors our interactions with other people. The term "psychological essentialism" refers to the belief that readily observable group differences are "immutable and naturally occurring," in the words of Chen and Ratliff. They continue that such beliefs "exacerbate intergroup biases by deepening and legitimizing perceived group differences." Psychological essentialism, according to them, has been linked to explicit prejudice but so far not to the implicit kind (Chen and Ratliff 2018, 303, 304), and their goal in this research was to show the link to both. Their results showed some effect in both, but only partially in implicit prejudice; in other words, the belief that differences between groups is natural, legitimate, and immutable is stronger with explicit prejudice than the implicit type, and that leads to stronger bias. Chen and Ratliff's findings also "suggest that psychological essentialism could be associated with stronger attitude generalization and reinforcement of those attitudes once formed" (2018, 317). Such categorical thinking thus leads to prejudice (e.g., Allport 1954; Gaertner et al. 2010, 528–530; Roets and Hiel 2011, 351) and is therefore a problematic orientation that makes overcoming negative prejudice more difficult. Stereotyping is a close cousin of psychological essentialism.

Introduced by Lippman (1922), the term "stereotype" refers to "the typical picture that comes to mind when thinking about a particular social group" (Dovidio et al. 2010, 7). As "cognitive moulds" (Brown 2010, 68), stereotypes "represent the traits that we view as characteristic of social groups, or of individual members of those groups, and particularly those that differentiate groups from each other" (Stangor 2009, 2). The key here is our perception, whether there is any truth in it or not. One attractive young woman, diabetic since childhood, described how someone said to her "You don't look diabetic," and she continued: "This jarring statement perpetuates an idea that rejects disability" (Smelter 2018). Most likely, the person meant to give the young woman a compliment, so why was it a negative, "jarring" statement? By assuming that diabetics have a certain distinguishing "look," the statement implies that a "normal-looking" person cannot be diabetic. Coates (2015, 116) gives another example of such "compliments" to his wife: "the people who thought they were white told her she was smart and followed this up by telling her she was not really black." For yet another example, I have sometimes heard a white parent say: "My son is married to a [member of an ethnic minority], but she is *very* nice; we couldn't love her more!" In other words, the ethnic group in question is identified negatively, but this daughter-in-law is an exception. Any member of an ethnic minority can testify that to be singled out as an exception in her or his ethnic group is not a compliment but rather a microaggression because it implies a negative stereotype of one's people.

Positive stereotypes, however, are also proven to be problematic, maybe even more so. Research has shown the ill effects of positive stereotypes, as when some groups are defined as "model minorities" (e.g., Cheryan and Bodenhausen 2000). In fact, positive stereotypes are shown to be even more harmful than not just the absence of stereotypes but also the presence of negative stereotypes. This is because positive stereotypes are often seen as "harmless" and even "flattering," so they may go "unnoticed and unchallenged." Yet they increase "essentialist beliefs" about biological differences between groups and thus have the "ability . . . to facilitate negative stereotyping" (Kay et al. 2013, 291), and they may impose an impossible standard for members of the group. Women are often recipients of positive stereotyping—for example, "nicer" than men, beautiful, nurturing, supportive, self-sacrificial, to be put on a pedestal, to be cherished and protected, and so forth. Such sugarcoated subordination often takes the form of paternalism or patronizing, "benevolent sexist" views that are equally pernicious as the hostile ones (e.g., Dovidio et al. 2010, 6; Brown 2010, 6–7; Kay et al. 2013, 288).

Stereotypes often contain "a grain of truth" (Brown 2010, 70) which is then unduly generalized. Stereotypical thinking isolates a certain characteristic that may be true of some members of the group and uses it to define the entire group. It is another example of categorization. The sociological term "master status" is a closely related concept in that it leads people to first see the category that the other person belongs to. For example, before anything else what she may be, a woman is first and foremost seen as a woman,[2] and a member of a racial minority is too often defined first and foremost with a racial category. Being initially defined by such a category or master status is stereotyping because it implies that the person meets certain characteristics believed to be typical of "such people," and it blinds the perceiver to the true qualities of the person. That kind of categorization prevents or delays recognition of the other as a unique person because it places that person in an outgroup (Gaertner et al. 2010, 528–530).

Stereotypes, however, help our perception by "simplifying a complex environment." They are "cognitive schemas used by social perceivers to process information about others" (Dovidio et al. 2010, 7, referring to Hilton and von Hippel 1996). Thus they are helpful in initially making sense of our perceptions, as Schutz also explained by his term "typification," discussed in chapter 1. Furthermore, recalling the discussion of interpersonal perception in chapter 2, all our perceptions occur in a larger context. According to Merleau-Ponty, "experience is organized at the most basic level by . . . 'preconceptual generalities,' and it is on the back of these generalities that empirical concepts are formed" (Antich 2018, 280). And Antich continues:

> In fact, there is no experience that is not already conceptualized within a field or horizon of other experiences and that does not accordingly already participate in generalities. . . . In other words, experience is a field, an open unity, in virtue at least of the open unity of space and time, such that every object in being experienced is not isolated but a part of a whole of experience. . . . [W]hat is really primary in experience are not facts or essences but such generalities or fields. Individuals are formed out of such generalities through a process of individuation or differentiation, rather than being the pregiven out of which we construct generalities. (Antich 2018, 285)

Interpersonal perception is no exception. Like natural objects, people also appear to us in a larger context: the environmental and cultural contexts coalesce in the personal, and, as explained in chapter 2, the perceiver's previous experiences form a part of that context. Thus every encounter involves some preconceived idea of what is in front of us that enables us to "individuate" or "differentiate" a specific object of perception. This partly depends on what Schutz termed our "stock of knowledge" (chapter 1) about the world around us. It is often inaccurate and always inadequate—perhaps only a hunch or a feeling about the thing, person, or situation that we face. But the more we objectively know about the person the less we rely on categorization and prejudgment. In meeting the other person as a unique being, Levinas notes, "I have overlooked the universal being he incarnates in order to confine myself to the particular being he is" (1998, 7). At any rate, because our understanding is colored by our previous experiences, knowledge, cultural and personal backgrounds and the structural context, our prejudice—the preconceived idea—is like a veil through which we see reality.

In addition, our perception is situated "within our life circumstance . . . a perspective that informs and enables" our reason (Sandel 2014, 3). These and many other factors form the basis on which we make a judgment—sometimes hastily; thus prejudice is a prejudgment. As Gadamer points out, "all understanding inevitably involves some prejudice," because "prejudice means a judgment that is given before all the elements that determine a situation have been finally examined" (1982, 239–240).[3] The task, then, is to "test" the prejudice, to "clarify the conditions in which understanding takes place" and separate the "productive prejudices that make understanding possible from the prejudices that hinder understanding and lead to misunderstandings" (Gadamer 1982, 178, 180, 263).

To briefly summarize, prejudice is an attitude toward someone on the basis of her or his group membership. It can be negative or positive, and explicit or implicit. Though efforts have been successful in reducing explicit prejudice, the implicit type is still prevalent. One example is the wide spectrum of microaggressions that members of marginalized groups experience on a daily basis. Because people engaging in them are not aware of their harmfulness, they often go unchallenged, but they have a negative effect on the self-esteem of those at the receiving end, leading them to not feeling at home in their home country. Stereotypical thinking is behind these and other implicit biases, and even positive stereotypes are harmful because they represent essentialist or categorical thinking. While such "typification" simplifies perception by providing a context, ethical approach toward other people requires seeing them as unique individuals.

A BRIEF HISTORY OF PREJUDICE

Definitions of prejudice have changed and simplified over the years. Prejudicial attitudes in both their negative and positive senses have been around as long as there have been people on Planet Earth; ingroups and outgroups, tribal warfare and other conflicts attest to that. In the Old Testament story of

Moses, his brother and sister criticized him for marrying a Cushite (Ethiopian) woman (Numbers 12:1). In classical Greece, slaves and women were considered lower level creatures that lacked reason. Although it was not named with the term prejudice, discussions of behaviors and attitudes that implied that were prevalent already in classical Greece.[4] Expositions on the meaning and source of reason and knowledge are instructive. As is well known, Plato and Aristotle had different conceptions of reason: for Plato, reason was abstract, detached from physical or social reality, whereas Aristotle's term *phronesis*, "practical wisdom," is "a corrective to the detached ideal of knowledge." It requires "an engaged understanding of the situation of action" (Sandel 2014, 20) that, as Sandel explains, is the correct understanding of prejudice that shows its necessity for understanding. Later Cicero, however, focused again on the negative definition, terming prejudice (*praeiusticium*) as "the opposite of truth, associated with error," born of manipulation (Steinbauer 2019).

The Enlightenment philosophers focused more on the negative meaning of the term because of the rise of scientific thinking in which prejudice was seen as incompatible with objectivity. In their detached conception of prejudice, both Bacon and Descartes wrote that the goal is to be unbiased, a "blank slate" (Bacon), "cleansed of prejudice" (Sandel 2014, 2, 24–25), staying clear of the "false mirror" of prejudice that distorts the truth (Steinbauer 2019, on Bacon). Then Immanuel Kant described prejudices as "preliminary opinions that are mistaken for final conclusions" (Steinbauer 2019) and defined the Enlightenment as "the emancipation from prejudices generally" (Kant 1952, 152). As Gadamer puts it, "the fundamental prejudice of the enlightenment is the prejudice against prejudice itself" (1982, 239–240).[5] Before and during the French Revolution, prejudice (*préjugé*) became "a fashionable term" as "a tool for condemning both religious tradition and the socio-political status quo," something that "could only be eradicated by means of the guillotine" (Steinbauer 2019).

Different voices began soon to be heard, however. During the French Revolution, Edmund Burke "championed 'prejudice' over 'naked reason,' on the grounds that prejudice contained the 'latest wisdom' of tradition and well-established habits." He was skeptical of reason, for him "the hubris of reason had led to the guillotine" (Badger 2010). Critical theorists of the Frankfurt School, such as its founders Adorno and Horkheimer (Tarr 2011), also blamed the Enlightenment for failing to provide moral understanding in its single-minded emphasis on reason. Thus for Adorno, "the Enlightenment journey led to Auschwitz and its gas chambers" (Badger 2010). Nietzsche and his postmodernist disciples, on their part, saw the Enlightenment as failing in philosophical courage by not fulfilling its potential of total liberation. Finally, "conservatives" and "communitarians" found a lot to criticize in Enlightenment thinking because with its individualism it ignored one's upbringing, the importance of community, and our embeddedness in the traditions and customs of our communities. For Gadamer, all understanding inevitably involves some prejudice, and Sandel (2014, 2–3) distinguishes between the "detached conception" of reason—objectivity according to Plato and in the Enlightenment sense—and the "situated conception" which is more true to life and necessarily involves prejudice. Aristotle is the forefather of this latter thinking, as explained by Sandel (above). [6]

In his classical and definitive work on prejudice, Allport traces a three-stage development in the meaning of this term: (1) to the ancients it was simply a precedent, "a judgment based on previous decisions and experiences"; (2) later it became "a judgment formed before due examination and consideration of the facts"; and finally (3) it acquired an additional "emotional flavor of favorableness or unfavorableness that accompanies such a prior and unsupported judgment" (1958, 7). After this sketch, however, and after acknowledging that we always have prejudice because we always have a preconceived idea of anything we perceive, he eventually settles on its negative meaning and goes on to discuss how we could lessen—if not completely eradicate—prejudicial attitudes. The negative definition has since become prevalent. For example, Webster's English dictionary defines prejudice first as an "unfavorable opinion or feeling formed beforehand and without knowledge, thought, or reason." A more general definition, however, appears as the second meaning: "any preconceived opinion or feeling, either favorable or unfavorable."

While prejudice has been around since time immemorial, understanding its meaning has changed and fluctuated over the years. The extreme emphasis on reason by the Enlightenment philosophers led to the negative definition that still holds sway today. Thus in today's understanding, there is a contradiction: there is a general agreement that we should have no prejudice in our human relationships, yet this cannot happen because all perceptions include some prejudgment, some orientation toward the thing to be perceived (Popper 1972, 345). If we understand prejudice in its full meaning with both positive and negative dimensions, we can solve the contradiction and begin to search for ways to enhance a positive prejudgment in our relationships.

FROM NEGATIVE TO POSITIVE PREJUDICE

To examine the possibility of "nonprejudice," Livingston (2011, 26) wonders "whether it is theoretically possible to be psychologically devoid of attitude and emotion," and whether such absence can be measured. Such a possibility would eliminate some of the human qualities from our interactions, so a negative answer seems obvious. Situational factors and emotions are present in all our perceptions. As the philosophy of critical realism asserts, there is such a thing as objective reality, but human perception of that reality is always incomplete and partial, so the same "facts" may look different to different people. People process information through their own filters, making total objectivity impossible (e.g., Kuhn 1996, 162; Derrida 1973; Ricoeur 1981, 62; Marton 1988, 179; Haraway 1988). Even the way we "know" certain facts means the way we interpret these facts, and that depends on what else we know and what our background is. This is what Sandel refers to as "situated understanding," and Gadamer states that it is only through our "shared horizons"—that is, our mutual existential situation as humans—that we understand one another at all.

When our "situated understanding," however, leads to negatively prejudiced or stereotyped approaches to other people, this has harmful consequences for the people at the receiving end. As discussed in chapter 1, our sense of self is derived from our association with others, thus a negatively perceived identity is devastating to self-esteem. Moreover, targets of prejudice often experience stress (Major and Townsend 2010, 413–414), and stigma[7] has been shown to lead to self-fulfilling prophecy, the tendency of people to behave according to the expectations of others (Brown 2010: 94–98, 219)—especially influential others, as the famous Rosenthal experiment showed with its discovery that students performed according to teacher expectations (Rosenthal and Jacobson 1968). Our "situational understanding" can also lead to "the soft bigotry of low expectations," a type of negative prejudice that shows when someone is praised for small, simple, inconsequential things while the greater things the person has done are ignored. That kind of praise has the opposite effect of dampening the receiving person's self-esteem.

While such "misrecognition" is ethically unwarranted and causes psychological harm (Honneth 1996, 2012), Fraser's "status model of recognition" focuses on objective forms of injustice "that prevent one from participating as a peer in social life." According to Fraser, such injustices are "externally manifest and publicly verifiable impediments to some people's standing as full members of society." These injustices are embedded in institutional practices that—as discussed in chapter 2—form the structural context of social interaction. As Fraser notes, remedying this requires "changing institutions and social practices," even "redistribution of resources and wealth" (Fraser and Honneth 2003, 29–33). Fraser's model focuses on overt economical discrimination that is an outcome of negative prejudice. Individual prejudicial attitudes held collectively, as well as institutionally established negative perceptions of groups, can lead to such undesirable objective outcomes to those at the receiving end.

Whether explicit or implicit, negative prejudicial attitudes are universally condemned, rightly so, and discussions largely focus on ways to remove them from our interpersonal association. Most efforts are aimed at prejudice

reduction, that is, the self-regulation or suppression of stereotypical or negative prejudicial beliefs. Guilt may be one motivation for the efforts that has
seemed to work (Jones 2002, 174). These efforts, however, have limitations;
if the attitudes are not strong the efforts may work to a certain extent, but
experiments have shown that efforts at suppression may actually make the
prejudicial attitudes stronger (Jones 2002, 171–174; Monteith et al. 2010,
496). Monteith and Mark's (2005, 510) comment provides a possible reason:
"Because it does not create a positive goal that one works toward but rather
places a focus on avoidance of unwanted thoughts and outcomes, this strate-
gy alone is not likely to prove effective in producing long-term changes to
the stereotypic and evaluative underpinnings of prejudiced responses even
among low-prejudice individuals."

It is unrealistic to simply try to remove an attitude without replacing it
with anything, as much of psychological literature has implored us to do.
Without "situated understanding" we cannot understand at all. But if "nonprejudice" is not possible, what is the solution? Livingston provides one by
suggesting "that it is possible to be functionally nonprejudiced even if one
cannot be nonprejudiced in an absolute (zero) sense" (2011, 26). A better
idea, however, is to enlarge our "situation"—to draw a wider circle—by
emphasizing similarities rather than differences. This can lead to a "universal
orientation" that integrates rather than differentiates self and others (Livingston 2011, 27). It means enlarging one's ingroup (Fehr 2010, 398), "creating
larger and more inclusive categories" (Brown 2010, 264–65). With "internal
motivation," that is, "a strong personal desire to avoid stereotypic thoughts"
(Monteith et al. 2010, 497) and a "personal dedication to responding without
prejudice" (Butz and Plant 2011, 94), such efforts may be more successful.

Contact with different groups has shown a "reliable" though not strong
relationship with reduction of negative prejudice (Brown 2010, 257). Because "contact goes below the surface, affecting non-conscious, automatic
processes," even "the willingness to trust and forgive" (Gaetner et al. 2010,
556), it helps people understand one another. Contact also facilitates empathy. As discussed in chapter 1, empathy means the ability to put oneself in
the shoes of another. The ability to see where the Other is coming from,
taking her perspective, will increase positive feelings toward that person. In
fact, "it may be possible merely to fantasize about a positive intergroup
interaction to effect some attitude change" (Brown 2010, 276). This means
creating a positive goal that focuses beyond the self (Migacheva et al 2011)
on a larger collectivity that includes both self and different others, rather than
merely removing a prejudicial attitude. While Livingston (2011, 27) offered
the "universal orientation" as an example of "nonprejudice," my suggestion
is that it changes prejudice from negative to positive because it draws the
Other into one's own circle. This, however, should not exclude the recognition of difference that usually is closely connected to the Other's identity. For

example, what is wrong with colorblindness is that with its "abstract universalism" it "ignores difference" (Bonilla-Silva 2017) and denies the identity of the Other in which color plays a definite role.

The key then is attitude change, something that is easier said than done. Prejudice (implying the negative type) toward people and groups we don't know, seems to be a "default" position in humans,[8] but evidence is "equally strong" that people also have positive values, such as "justice, fairness, and cooperation." Whether these values can override negative prejudice is the burning question; such efforts may have led to "modern prejudice," such as "symbolic racism" or "subtle racism" (Livingston 2011, 24), examples of the implicit types of prejudice discussed above. Cognitively acknowledging the good qualities of the other individual or group may still not easily lead to positive affective orientations. Interpreting Hegel, Honneth (2012, 15) describes a respectful interpersonal situation as one where "both sides are compelled to restrict their self-seeking drives." At best, this is a process of self-development, "the purposeful pursuit of the real human telos [that], far from being easy, demands a life-long struggle, serious learning, and continual effort to work against countervailing forces" (Christian Smith 2010, 401).

To begin the process of changing one's attitude requires first understanding oneself, one's own background, and honestly acknowledging one's feelings; "awareness of one's implicit biases is a good and healthy first step for the effortful control of prejudiced reactions" (Hahn et al. 2014, 1388, citing Monteith and Mark 2005). This means seeing oneself objectively (Mead's "me," see chapter 1). Once we thus understand our own attitude, we have taken the most important step toward shaping it in a positive direction. But time is of the essence: "what happens *immediately* after the automatic activation of a stereotype is indeed under our control" (Jones 2002, 21, emphasis hers, citing Fiske [1992] and Dovidio et al. [1997]). It means engaging in an internal conversation between the "I" and the "me" (Mead), catching oneself—"Oops!"—and listening to one's superego that is bringing in the internalized moral values, according to Freud. While "typification," stereotyping, and other "cognitive schemas" have helped us make some sense of the perception, that has involved our prejudicial "id" and thus often stands in need of correction.

The apparent is not the true picture; "the 'real' is to be discovered beyond the immediate" (Sohn 2014, 23, discussing Levinas). Merleau-Ponty's phenomenology of perception also points that out: raw perception is like an illusion or mythical thinking, unreflected, colored by hearsay, that is wrong to be taken as truth. Instead, we can "displace one *cogito* in favor of another, and to meet up with the truth of my thought beyond its appearance" (Merleau-Ponty 2012, 311). This assumes that we have internalized the best values of our society, embraced what Abraham Lincoln called "the better angels of our nature." An attitude transformation from negative to positive can take place when our agency calls forth our values of fairness and kindness and our ethical belief in the inherent worth of all human beings. It is a correction to an illusion.

There are situations in which positive prejudice comes to the fore quite easily: we are automatically positively prejudiced toward people we identify with. Thus the enlarged ingroup is key. However, at this juncture it needs to be reiterated that positive prejudice is not to be equated with positive stereotypes as sometimes seems implied. The "superficially positive" ideas about women (Brown 2010, 6), for example, as always having to be beautiful, or praised for trivial things, is stereotyping with its above-described negative effects. All stereotypes are about outgroups, they are perceptions of an Other whom we don't know enough to have an accurate understanding. A positively prejudiced person will acknowledge what she doesn't know. As discussed in chapter 1, the other person is totally Other, so the best we can do is to give him the benefit of the doubt. This is actually what the United States' criminal justice system is supposed to do by the rule that the accused is to be assumed innocent until proven guilty.

Various specific efforts to create positive prejudice are not uncommon. When we introduce a friend to someone, we may praise her to create a positive impression, and when an unknown speaker is introduced to an audience his qualifications are listed and sometimes amplified to a superhuman level, so the audience will be favorably disposed toward him. That creates respect and positive expectations and these, in turn, give the speaker more confidence and inspiration. Expectation is not to be equated with prejudice as Dorschel (2000, 60) claims Gadamer does. These are related but not the same. Expectation is what I expect to hear from the speaker; prejudice has to do with my perception of him, whether I see him as an authority on the subject, for example. A positive introduction creates trust in the speaker so that the audience will be favorably disposed toward him and his message and will interpret the message positively. We have high expectations toward those we respect, though the expectations are the result and not the meaning of prejudice.

To be positively disposed toward other people means respecting them, expecting them to be good and competent individuals. The subtle, unspoken evaluations—before verbal communication takes place—are positive and affirming. At a very basic level, recognition of belonging to the same human family facilitates "merging our horizons" (in Gadamer's words) which makes mutual understanding possible. It is identification. Positive prejudice also means openness and willingness to see the world from the viewpoint of the other—as much as that is possible, for one's own sake and the Other's. Psychologists have shown that most of us have a "confirmation bias" (Nickerson 1998); we are drawn to ideas that confirm our own. To be open and respectful to people and ideas that differ from ours is prejudice in its positive sense.

At one time, when I talked about positive prejudice in class, a student remarked: "it's curiosity-based." Somehow that didn't seem right to me, though only later I realized why: as discussed earlier, curiosity is a desire to satisfy one's urge to know, thus it is focusing on oneself; genuine interest in the other person—which I see as congruent with positive prejudice—is focusing on that person, for that person's sake. It is "*the superlative moral priority of the other person . . .* , according to which being 'for-the-other' takes precedence over, is better than, being for-itself" (Cohen 2003, xxvi, on Levinas's philosophy, emphasis his). Positive prejudice tries to understand the other person on her own terms, and when understanding is inadequate, it respects the otherness of the Other, the fact that she is an independent moral agent who is different from oneself. It means assuming the unknown person is good, and proceeding with that assumption until the person proves otherwise. Negative prejudice is the opposite.

Understanding prejudice in its negative sense and focusing on its removal has been the traditional approach because social sciences generally have focused on problems. Lately, however, there is a new trend in them that focuses on the desirable rather than the problematic. In sociology, for example, altruism traditionally received little attention but has since become a valued area of study (Simmons 1991).[9] And "positive psychology" (e.g., Mikulincer and Shaver 2010) has been around for some years. Representing this new trend, Tropp and Mallett's (2011) edited book, *Moving Beyond Prejudice Reduction*, includes articles on topics like positive attitudes (Pittinsky et al. 2011), motivations (Butz and Plant), positive goal orientations (Migacheva el al. 2011), friendship (Davies et al. 2011; Page-Gould and Mendoza-Denton 2011) and forgiveness (Swart et al. 2011). These topics show an appreciation for the value of a positive orientation. The new studies do not advocate freedom from prejudice but the possibility of its positive forms that we can actively work toward by practicing fairness and kindness that can become a positive force in society.

For one more notable example of the increasing attempts at turning the emphasis in studies of social interaction in a positive direction, at the University of California in Los Angeles, an interdisciplinary center, the UCLA Bedari Kindness Institute, opened in 2019. The press release describes its purpose as follows: "The institute, which is housed in the division of social sciences, will support world-class research on kindness, create opportunities to translate that research into real-world practices, and serve as a global platform to educate and communicate its findings. Among its principal goals are to empower citizens and inspire leaders to build more humane societies." The institute "will focus on research about the actions, thoughts, feelings and social institutions associated with kindness," the description continues. The inaugural director, anthropologist Daniel Fessler, has been studying kindness and its effect on "uplifting emotional experience that in turn motivates the observer to be kind" (Abraham 2019). Earlier experiments have also shown that "participants who were treated kindly showed a positivity bias compared with participants who were treated unkindly" (Livingston 2011, 32). Thus addressing the "better angels of our nature" has far-reaching consequences for shaping society in a positive direction.

TOLERATION AND RECOGNITION

Tolerance or toleration has traditionally been held as a goal in ethnic relations. Though the term has thus been seen in a positive light, my claim is that it does not come close to positive prejudice but may involve the negative type. Positive prejudice involves recognition rather than mere toleration. Indeed, tolerance has lately acquired negative connotations. Dictionaries define tolerance in following ways: "sympathy or indulgence of beliefs or practices different from one's own" (Webster), or "the ability or willingness to tolerate the existence of opinions or behaviors that one dislikes or disagrees with" (Oxford). Ben-Zeev (2009) discusses tolerance in relation to some deviant behavior of other people in which one nevertheless sees some positive feature important enough that it needs to be tolerated. He states that tolerance is "closer to intellectual reasoning than to emotions," and therefore "overcomes emotional values." Tolerance then is a rational decision when emotions would lead the intolerant to different responses. For example, people who are vehemently opposed to abortion, homosexuality, women or racial minorities in leadership positions, or other behaviors, practices, or identities that differ from the mainstream, may be emotionally led to some overt action, even violence. Tolerance would mean accepting such "deviance" as part of society, even grudgingly. Or it may involve merely "a symbolic recognition of differences" (Galeotti 2002, 101).

Mere tolerance could also mean an attitude of avoidance rather than appreciation or desire to include the different people or groups in one's own circle. Reflecting on a "restricted definition" of the term, Galeotti (2002, 225, 226) writes that tolerance is sometimes "equated to indifference," and even an "attitude implying double negation: first, a negative appraisal of some forms of behavior or practices of others, and second, a decision not to interfere with it." He notes that "toleration includes a whole range of meanings: forbearing, putting up with, permitting, accepting, recognizing." Tolerance has been acknowledged as a low level of acceptance of others (e.g., Allport 1954) that would seem cold and uncaring at best (Ben-Zeev 2009). But Allport laments that the English language does not have a better word, and goes on discussing tolerance as a goal anyway. Use of the word seems to be waning, however. Apparently because of its less than positive connotation, the word does not appear in the subject index of many recent books on prejudice (e.g., Jones 2002; Brown 2010; Dovidio et al. 2010). It seems the new emphasis on positive psychology has caused the word to fall out of fashion in psychological literature. Chugh (2018, 154–55) writes that "tolerance otherizes difference." The term may be more appropriate when applied to groups rather than to individuals, though even then it is not an ideal form of acceptance.

At a fundamental level in the society at large, tolerance would be needed for groups that are in some ways different from the dominant culture—to live and let live—and it is indeed inherent in democratic human rights. Galeotti (2002, 1) states: ". . . in liberal democracies toleration is generally recognized as the ethically proper means of accommodating differences in values and lifestyles." And he continues:

> The inclusion of the ideal of toleration in constitutional rights as a means of protecting individual freedom of conscience, expression, and association seems to render the very notion of tolerance superfluous. If everyone is granted the right to entertain and to pursue his or her own conception of the good and its corresponding lifestyle, as long as no harm to any third party is produced, the state has no right to tolerate any different behavior, ideas or morality, since it has no right to "tolerate" (in the strict sense) what it has no entitlement to forbid in the first place. (Galeotti 2002, 2, referring to Thomas Paine)

Democratic values, such as multiculturalism and equal rights, already include tolerance, so it no longer should need to be emphasized. According to Kant (1991, 58), a prince who allows complete freedom to his subjects and "thus even declines to accept the presumptuous title of tolerant is himself enlightened." Noble as that may be, in today's world such "enlightenment" is not sufficient. Racism and other "isms" may "tolerate" different groups since it is the law, but such attitude implies a superior position, looking down on the "tolerated" others. Members of such groups will then feel keenly their unequal status. The need for recognition rather than mere toleration is evident in the refrain "I am somebody!" during the Civil Rights Movement. African Americans had so long been invisible in the society as persons; now they claimed personhood, recognition.

Nevertheless, some commentators—including philosophers—see tolerance as an entirely positive attitude, in fact a moral virtue (Witenberg 2014), and it has been equated with recognition (Galeotti 2002; Apel 1997). In a legal sense this may work, but human needs go beyond legal rights. As introduced in chapter 1, Honneth (1996) describes three spheres in human life where recognition is needed, where indeed demand for it is a "struggle." A baby needs love, not mere toleration; that need continues through life and when fulfilled, the individual gains self-confidence. As Ricoeur notes, its absence is disregard and humiliation that makes the individual feel "looked down from above, even taken as insignificant" (Ricoeur 2005, 191).

In the public sphere, Honneth's second category, people need to be recognized as citizens with the rights pertaining to that status, such as voting rights. While members of various minority groups have been "tolerated" in such a manner over the years, especially if they blend in the dominant culture (e.g., the "Don't ask don't tell!" approach toward sexual minorities), that level of acceptance results in invisibility and leads to stigma and its concomitant negative feelings. Galeotti (2002, 12) explains: "Given the public invisibility of their identity and its social stigmatization, self-esteem is often pursued at the price of rejecting difference, resulting in humiliation and the loss of self-respect." Toleration, then, "is a virtue if it promotes mutual respect and social cooperation and allows people to deal with conflicts peacefully," and "as recognition is aimed at making people, whatever their differences and identities, feel at ease with themselves, and at ease with their choice to identify with certain differences" (Galeotti 2002, 225, 227). Recognition is generally gained by the "struggle" of social movements (e.g., Civil Rights, Gay Rights), and receiving it strengthens the group members' self-respect.

In the social sphere, the third in Honneth's exposition, I would see mere tolerance as misrecognition, that is, the person's right to exist but not counted on for any valuable contribution and thus left in the periphery. Yet, as Honneth asserts, every person needs recognition in some community as a good and capable individual with unique characteristics and talents and thus with positive contributions to make, and such recognition yields self-esteem. Accordingly, Ricoeur (2005, 21) considers identity recognition as a "culminating point" that "demands to be recognized."

It is clear then that recognition goes far beyond toleration, and Ricoeur considers it "more important" than identity in multiculturalism (Ricoeur 1998, 60, quoted by Sohn 2014, 133): "In the notion of identity there is only the idea of sameness; whereas recognition is a concept that directly integrates otherness and allows a dialectic of the same and the other. The demand for identity always involves something violent with respect to others. On the contrary, the search for recognition implies reciprocity." Without reciprocity, Ricoeur observes that the demand for recognition can be endless and may result in "an insatiable sense of victimization" (Sohn 2014, 133). Reciprocity means mutual recognition—members habitually recognizing one another without a "struggle," and that strengthens the bonds of belonging in a community. While Ricoeur accepts Honneth's (and Hegel's) idea of the need for recognition as a "struggle," he offers a "peaceful alternative" and "a deeper and fuller understanding of recognition" (Sohn 2014, 136). Ricoeur illustrates the mutuality involved with the idea of a gift, with the "phenomenology of the gift" (Ricoeur 2005, 241–243).

In his extended discussion of motivations involved in gift-giving and gift-exchange as models of recognition, Ricoeur rules out *agape* with its self-denial (Ricoeur 2005, 220–25) and thus complements Levinas's one-sided sacrifice for the other (Sohn 2014, 136). Likewise, he rejects the economic model of gift-exchange (Ricoeur 2005, 225–32)—explicated by Marcel Mauss (1967)—as well as "abstract universalism" that is "'blind to differences' in the name of liberal neutrality" (Ricoeur 2005, 214). His "phenomenology of intentions," locates the return of a gift as "a response to a call coming from the generosity of the first gift." In fact, gratitude is already such a return gift, "which is the soul of the division between good and bad reciprocity" (Ricoeur 2005, 243). Mutual spirit of generosity grants recognition to others in the context of a relationship. Ricoeur sees this as a journey or "course" that begins with self-recognition and extends to others:

> This, in broad strokes, is the dynamic I could begin to call a "course" of recognition becomes apparent—I mean the passage from recognition-identification, where the thinking subject claims to master meaning, to mutual recognition, where the subject places him- or herself under the tutelage of a relationship of reciprocity, in passing through self-recognition in the variety of capacities that modulate one's ability to act, one's "agency." (Ricoeur 2005, 248)

A person's agency is developed in relationships, as discussed in chapter 1. And at each stage of the lifecycle one needs recognition in the forms of love, civil rights, and appreciation in a community. Positive prejudice is the healthy underlying attitude that facilitates such recognition.

The "struggle" for recognition, however, can also lead to antisocial behavior. Every parent knows that children can misbehave in order to get attention, and Honneth suspects "that Hegel traces the emergence of crime to conditions of incomplete recognition." With "the established stage of mutual recognition," not being recognized can become a motive for criminal behavior (1996, 20). It is one means, though unhealthy, for remedying the view of oneself as insignificant and thus gaining some self-esteem. The bravado of many a gang member is no doubt motivated by such struggle for recognition.

Clearly, positive prejudice includes recognition of the value and contributions of different groups and their members. And as Ricoeur shows in his "peaceful" model of mutual recognition, one must recognize both oneself and others, and when others recognize one it is easier to recognize oneself. Thus mutuality is at the core, and when such recognition is widespread it can create an overall positive atmosphere in society. Mere toleration may include a negatively prejudiced attitude, but positive prejudice that goes far beyond toleration is needed for true recognition that enhances the self-esteem of those at the receiving end.

CONCLUSION

The concept of prejudice is active in public consciousness, and the more ethnic and other diversity there is in society the more attention to it is needed. The term, however, is often narrowly conceived as a negative attitude that one should reduce if not eliminate entirely. This review of the concept was an attempt to place it in a larger context as a general prejudgment that includes either negative or positive meanings. Prejudice is an attitude that includes cognitive and affective elements and can manifest itself explicitly or implicitly, the negative form of the latter being even more problematic than the former because of its hidden nature. Prejudice is involved in all our interactions because our understanding is always situated in our life circumstance and our social, historical, and personal context. Prejudice is related to stereotypes that are initially helpful in perception but can become problematic in interpersonal situations even when they are positive.

A brief historical sketch showed that prejudice has not always been a negative concept. Models of detached and situated understanding of reason are evident in the writings of Plato and Aristotle, respectively, the latter providing a basis for a positive meaning of the concept of prejudice. In their quest for scientific objectivity, Enlightenment thinkers gave prejudice its recent, prevalent negative meaning. Thus efforts have focused on reducing or eliminating prejudice, though it is impossible to rid oneself of attitudes and emotions. Rather, the challenge is to change prejudice from a negative to a positive attitude by becoming aware of one's negative attitude, by quickly correcting one's initial perception, by enlarging one's circle of identification, and by calling forth one's higher values of justice, fairness, and kindness. The chapter ends with a review of the concepts of toleration and recognition, the latter involving positive prejudice as its foundation.

Prejudice, in all its forms, is alive and well in the world. Its negative manifestations hardly need to be reiterated, but thankfully its positive forms are evident as well. These involve appreciation of others for who they are in their own right and an attitude of openness and humility that acknowledges the good qualities of people we don't know well or with whom we may disagree. Positive prejudice is the basis for recognition and respect, the subject of the next chapter.

NOTES

1. In many discussions, as here, prejudice and bias appear to be equated. That seems justified as Microsoft dictionary defines bias as an unfair "inclination or prejudice." Major and Townsend (2010, 410) describe how people manage with stigmatization, negative stereotypes, prejudice, and discrimination as "coping with bias."

2. It has been observed that men generally classify women in one of six categories: a wife or a girlfriend, a mother, a daughter, a sister, a whore, or an angel or saint (not necessarily in that order). I thank Nancy Hess for bringing this observation to my attention.

3. Dorschel claims that Gadamer equates prejudice with expectation, a stance he criticizes (2000, 60). His criticism notwithstanding, he makes the same point as Gadamer: "perhaps a prejudice is a judgment that does not take into account *enough* experience. On this account, prejudice would be a hasty generalization" (2000, 26, emphasis his).

4. As Dorschel explains, the word for prejudice does not occur in classical Greek before 300 BC. Not until the 18th century was the attitude of "misanthropy" seen "as a general explanation of prejudice" (2000, 26).

5. Dorschel again disagrees with Gadamer's claim about Enlightenment's "prejudice against prejudice." He says that Enlightenment sees judgment and prejudice as antithesis: "Judgment means coming to a conclusion after considering all the factors, while prejudice implies jumping to a conclusion without considering them." However, "there will never be a time when all the factors have been considered," thus there is selection, and "it must be a prejudice that singles out the relevant factors" (2000, 52, 53).

6. Badger (2010) disagrees with Aristotle and his modern "conservative" and "communitarian" interpreters, such as MacIntyre, Sandel, and others. He supports a modified understanding of individualism with its roots in the Enlightenment.

7. Phelan et al. (2008) consider stigma and prejudice as parts of the same larger concept, though stigma appears to refer to things like personal deviance, illness, or some physical characteristic, whereas prejudice is mostly used in the context of race relations. My suggestion is that stigma seems to be attached to the target person and may lead to negative prejudice, an attitude held by another regardless of the target characteristics.

8. Gladwell (2019), however, shows by his case studies that we tend to be too trusting of strangers. His examples seem to indicate the need for caution when dealing with strangers. My point, however, is that caution need not be negative. One can respect while keeping a distance.

9. The American Sociological Association (ASA) has a section on Altruism, Morality, and Social Solidarity, which shows that there is ongoing research in this area of study.

Chapter Four

Respect

We know in practice when we experience respect and when we don't. I will illustrate this with a recent personal experience. I was viewing the displays at a craft fare in Charleston, South Carolina. At some booths there were women weaving reef baskets that were for sale. Stopping to admire the handiwork at one such booth and seeing two African American women working on their weaving, I casually asked: "How long does it take for you to weave a basket like that?" Probably an inappropriate question, but my intention was friendliness, though I confess curiosity was part of it. Without answering my question, one of the women looked at me and said "Good morning." I responded to the greeting and somehow felt rebuked that I had not greeted her first. She proceeded then to give somewhat of an answer, like "it depends." Obviously the lady felt that I had no right to ask her a question without greeting her first and thus acknowledging her human dignity. And with my curiosity I committed the same offense people do when the first words they say to a person with a foreign accent are "Where are you from?" with no previous or further interaction. My casual approach did not make the lady feel respected as a person, though I had not intended any disrespect.

You may recall from chapter 2 Talcott Parsons' three elementary components of a system of action: cognition, cathexis, and evaluation. Cathexis means the emotional component. My question to the weaving lady was mainly cognitive, to satisfy my curiosity, though the affective component was implicit in it also as interest in the art of basket weaving. I forgot the interpersonal affective component that had the potential for her to feel respected. My evaluation of the interaction ignored that element of human need, and to her credit she had self-respect and calmly reminded me that she deserved respect. In ignoring her humanity, I had objectified her as simply an instrument that brings about the baskets; by demanding the respect that I did not initially give her, she transformed the occasion into a proper social interaction and taught me an important lesson.

This chapter delves into the issue of respect, what it means and how it shows in various interactions. My claim is that positive prejudice includes respect and is the basis for respect, and it is specifically about respecting the person or group that we know little about or with whom we don't agree. But what it means to respect another person is not as clear as it may seem on the surface. Often well-intended words or actions do not translate to a feeling of being respected on the part of the recipient, as my example illustrates. And as discussed in the previous chapters, how people experience social interactions makes a big difference for their sense of self, their confidence and their motivations. Microaggressions, for example, cause stress and psychological harm (Sue 2010a; Nadal 2014, 2), no doubt because such interactions are not respectful.

Ethics requires each of us to think about how our communications and actions affect the other, and to behave in a way that facilitates a positive interpersonal experience for others. Discussing Levinas, Sohn puts the subject of this chapter in a clear perspective: "Beyond the naturalistic principle that begins with *facts* within the world, beyond the phenomenological principle that begins with the constitution of *objects* within intentional consciousness, there is an ethical principle—the principle of all principles—which begins with the *other*" (2014, 126, emphasis Sohn's). Our approach toward the Other has been my focus throughout this book. The present chapter is intended to illuminate some of the factors that translate into respect versus disrespect for the recipient of the action, and what positive prejudice has to do with it.

THE MEANING OF AND BASIS FOR RESPECT

Some of the related concepts that come to mind in connection with respect are terms like regard, deference, honor, esteem, even admiration. Many of these terms imply a hierarchy in which those at higher levels expect to receive deference from those below, and those below generally grant it. Even though the American society claims to be egalitarian, hierarchy does exist here as well, though it is not as formal or explicit as in more traditional societies. My concern in this chapter, however, is not on that kind of respect but the kind that is due to every human being simply by virtue of being human. As Wuthnow observes, this kind of respect shows in relationships among persons of equal status, and is related to but not to be equated with trust: "Trust is an expectation based on past performance in role-specific activities, whereas respect refers to an assessment of the more diffuse qualities of persons" (2017, 20–21). Since it is humanity itself that deserves such respect, however, it must manifest itself not only between people of equal status but also mutually between people of unequal status.

My underlying assumption is that human beings possess dignity, and that is the basis for respect. Dignity is often equated with appropriate pride and self-esteem, as the basket-weaving lady exhibited by demanding respect from me. But it involves a more fundamental conception of what it means to be human and why humans deserve respect simply by virtue of belonging to the human family. The philosophy of personalism addresses that; it sees humans as persons and thus "something qualitatively more than and different from what many alternative views [e.g., the purely biological, economic, or political conceptions] construe humans to be" (Christian Smith 2010, 102). Personalism expresses "a belief in the primordial uniqueness of the human being, and thus in the basic irreducibility of the human being to the natural world" (Smith 2010, 104, quoting Wojtyla 2008, 211).

A philosophical treatise on respect by Kristi Giselsson is based on similar philosophy, although she does not use the word personalism. For her, "communal accountability . . . defines that which is human."[1] It "suggests that the human community is essentially a moral community, therefore giving human being a significance that is beyond the biological," and it "has to do with our *way* of being" (Giselsson 2012, 185, 186, 196, emphasis hers). Thus, as Christian Smith summarizes, human dignity is "ontologically real, analytically irreducible, and phenomenologically apparent"; it is an "inalienable" and "objective feature of human personhood," thus "a property of personhood that calls for self-realization through the recognition and honoring the dignity of other persons" (2010, 434, 443, 463).[2] Both Smith and Giselsson affirm that this philosophy does not necessitate belief in the supernatural.[3]

A major philosophical justification for respect for human dignity is found in the writings of Immanuel Kant. In his "formula of the Kingdom of Ends," Kant refers to the law that each person should "treat himself and all others, *never merely as a means*, but always *at the same time as an end in himself*" (Kant 1964, 101, emphasis his). In a commentary on Kant, O'Neill (1989) explains that to use another person as mere means is to view him or her as a thing or a prop, not a person. It is to use others to achieve one's own ends and not theirs. Kant acknowledges that by necessity we do use other people for our own ends, in commerce or in accepting favors or services, for example, but the point is to remember the other person's humanity and thus not treat him as *mere* means but *at the same time* as an end. In other words, the services were not rendered by a machine but by a human being with feelings and dignity.

Kant's point was forgotten in the practice of slavery, and—apart from its concrete cruelty—that is one reason why slavery is such an evil. In a particularly poignant passage, Coates drives home the humanity of a slave:

> Slavery is not an indefinable mass of flesh. It is a particular, specific enslaved woman, whose mind is active as your own, whose range of feelings is as vast as your own; who prefers the way the light falls in one particular spot in the woods, who enjoys fishing where the water eddies in a nearby stream, who loves her mother in her own complicated way, thinks her sister talks too loud, has a favorite cousin, a favorite season, who excels at dressmaking and knows, inside herself, that she is as intelligent and capable as anyone. (Coates 2015, 69–70)

In some forms, slavery still exists in the world, and even when a person gets paid for her services we may forget the human being who renders these services. As Smith explains, treating a person as a "thing" turns a "you" into an "it," and thus denies the personhood of that person. Things and human beings "belong to two different ontological orders of reality" and thus have different characteristics and moral dimensions (Christian Smith 2010, 436).

In an insightful article more than half a century ago, Maclagan (1960, 193–217) searches for a philosophical foundation for the commonly accepted principle—also from Kant—that "persons are to be respected, simply as persons." In the next few paragraphs, I will briefly summarize Maclagan's major points as he ponders why it should be so. He observes that it is a question of social morality, but justice is inadequate as a model because impartiality would rather mean the absence of respect. The fact that people have rational will and thus can make moral choices also falls short; it would lead one to expect the eradication of all corruption, which obviously is not the case. Furthermore, the mere existence of rational will is an awe-inspiring mystery, but such awe is directed at the mystery and does not necessarily lead to respect of the people who possess rational will.

Maclagan goes on to discuss friendship in light of Aristotle's analysis of it. To Maclagan, friendship provides "a clue" to respect because it acknowledges the importance of the person who matters in himself. It involves an unconcern with one's own position and partiality toward the other, which is moral. But friendship is based on mutual liking; respect cannot depend on liking, it "must be related to the simple 'thatness' not the 'suchness' of persons" (1960, 203). In addition, friendship fails as a model because it is not necessarily permanent. Love as romantic passion is concerned for the other "simply as being and not as being *such*" (1960, 204), so it would seem better, but it is irrational and too exclusive as a model for respect.[4]

Respect for persons must be based on rational will, Maclagan asserts. Love must be involved, but romantic love is "but a shadow" of the kind of love needed. He concludes that love in the biblical meaning of Agape fulfills the requirement, though he disassociates himself from the "orthodox Christian" use of the word. Agape is volitional and stable, "incorporating the *positive* valuation of persons as such that underlies the *comparative* valuation involved in justice," in a way that is "wholly outward-looking" and thus justifies the moral concern for others. Thus, "it is *in* Agape and in nothing less than that, that the principle of respect comes to life and breathes" (1960, 206–7; emphasis Maclagan's).

But without theological justification, where does Agape get its moral force? To answer this, Maclagan refers to Kant's "categorical imperative": *"Act only on that maxim through which you can at the same time will that it should become a universal law"* (Kant 1964, 88, emphasis his). A maxim is a principle that guides our actions. Agape is a maxim that is "a fact of experience," and its "rational factor consists in our general consciousness of obligation, the awareness that there are or may be claims upon us that run counter to our wishes and that have an authority" over us. Human beings have an innate capacity for this consciousness, and one of its functions is "to remove the psychological obstacle to Agape that is created by our natural self-centeredness and self-concern" (Maclagan 1960, 209–10). In addition to this rational factor, Agape includes a "natural" factor, our capacity for sympathy, and this is likewise part of our human endowment.

Maclagan (1960, 210–11) distinguishes three different meanings of sympathy. First, "animal sympathy" is a sort of "psychological infection," atmosphere that is created from infection of one creature by another, such as fear of something.[5] The second meaning of sympathy is more specifically human: "an imaginative 'feeling oneself into' the experience of the other, an emotional identification." Maclagan calls that empathy or a passive mode of human sympathy. This requires "escape from the obsession with ourselves." The third meaning, active human sympathy, is practical concern for the Other, and that is close to Agape. Passive sympathy is a necessary condition for the practical concern, and is so intertwined with it that "it is psychologically impossible genuinely to sympathize with anyone in the passive mode without at the same time having *some* measure of active sympathy also" (1960, 2012, emphasis Maclagan's).

But because this is purely natural, it is not yet moral, Maclagan continues. "Agape proper . . . is just precisely the reflective, 'principled' (and therewith moralized) version of this active sympathy" (1960, 16). This involves obligation, which is the rational factor and elevates the other person to moral importance. Respect for persons is almost like Agape, Maclagan concludes; its similarity with Agape gives it "the warmth of attitude." He summarizes that respect for persons is a fusion of active natural sympathy and rational will, a "moralized concern," moralized by our general consciousness of a moral obligation. It is just about like Agape but can be thought of without the "additional significance" that Christians attribute to Agape.

Kant's philosophy and the ethical principle of respect for persons have not gone without criticism. Green (2010, 213), for example, worries about "the difficulty of explaining" respect for persons and calls viewing it as simply a duty "a debunking explanation." And he notes that something that terminates on the person leaves out a reason why persons should be respected.[6] Similarly, Honneth (1996, 172) observes that the Kantian tradition "is unable to locate the purpose of morality as a whole within the concrete goals of human subjects." In a departure from this tradition he focuses on the conditions for humans' "self-realization." Thus "morality, understood as the point of view of universal respect, becomes one of several protective measures that serve the general purpose of enabling the good life"—including structures that accept a plurality of forms of life, making "human self-realization as an end" (1996, 173). Another problem with Kant's philosophy is its reliance on reason, as Giselsson (2012) points out: if respect is only given to those who have reason, it will leave out those with inadequate reason, such as infants, brain-injured, and demented people. Her answer to this dilemma is emphasizing the communal aspect of respect: such people are part of the human moral community, and it is the community that is accountable for them when they themselves cannot be.

Respect for the other is also at the heart of the writings of Levinas. As observed in the first chapter, he has combined phenomenology and ethics with focus on the face-to-face encounter. He emphasizes the fact that the other person is not a phenomenon but has independent existence; "in our relation to the other, the latter does not affect us by means of a concept. The other is a being and counts as such" (1998, 5). Conceivably, to think of the other as a phenomenon would make that person a thing and thus objectify her. There is a difference between our relation to objects and our relation to being: "the person with whom I am in relation, I call being, but in calling him *being*, I call upon him" (Levinas 1998, 7, emphasis his). There is more to a person than some entity that we need to truly see, even appreciate. As Levinas asserts, the Other has a demand on us, and that is where ethics enters the picture.

As discussed in chapter 1, our self is established and maintained through social contacts. But this need is fulfilled only if we feel respected in these contacts, and respect means that each person is a subject rather than an object. However, as Giselsson and others have observed, Levinas's ideas— like Kant's and other Enlightenment philosophers'—are an abstraction: "such a mystical and abstract conception of the human face leaves the lives of actual, concrete humans exceedingly difficult to grasp, and this is directly due to the lack of situated particularity in Levinas's notion of the face" (Giselsson 2012, 48). Concrete situations of human beings are the setting in all interactions in which people need to be respected and need to give respect to others. This was also the criticism of social philosophies given by Dorothy Smith (1987), referred to in chapter 1. That means respect cannot remain only at the level of lip service but demands concrete action.

To summarize this section, justification for the philosophical demand for respect for persons rests on the unique nature of human beings: our ontological existence and uniqueness that sets us apart from the rest of the natural world, and on the human need for self-realization that respect helps bring about. The philosophical perspective of personalism acknowledges this unique nature of humans. Kant's philosophy, furthermore, provides important insights for the ethics of respect with its insistence that humans need to be treated by others as ends in themselves and not mere means. Despite criticisms, most discussions on respect take Kant's philosophy as a starting point. And as discussed in previous chapters, respectfully sharing the horizons with other humans is positive prejudice.

RECOGNITION AS RESPECT

I have mentioned the philosophical concept of recognition several times earlier, yet it needs to be taken up again because of its close affinity with respect and positive prejudice. Honneth's three spheres in which recognition is needed—our needs for love, acknowledgment in society at large and affirmation in our social circles (see chapter 3)—have to do with our need for respect. According to Ricoeur, "an ethics of respect is the proper grounding for . . . Hegelian phenomenology of struggles for recognition" (Sohn 2014, 82). My example at the beginning of this chapter shows the need in our daily interactions to be recognized as dignified human beings, and when we are positively prejudiced we give such recognition. Expecting it shows self-respect, and giving it is respecting others.

The first two spheres of recognition that Honneth identifies do indeed coincide with respect as discussed above: love that does not come from respect is not love, and respect for citizens in the public sphere demands not only that they have equal rights—whether voting or other rights—but also that they are recognized as independent moral agents with their own goals, preferences and feelings that no-one has the right to violate. Honneth's third sphere, however, demands "a suitable rational, moral response to the *evaluative* qualities of human beings" (Honneth 2012, 92, emphasis mine). Honneth often refers to achievements as the basis for such recognition, and that distinguishes it from the kind of universal respect that is my focus here.

In the Kantian sense, respect is due to people by mere virtue of their being human, not because of any particular qualities the person possesses. How can we reconcile this with Honneth's idea of communal recognition? The answer lies in positive prejudice that leads us to see the positive qualities of every person and to expect such qualities; recognizing these is showing respect to the person. Thus even this sphere may be seen as based on respect. Recognizing someone for whatever reason does involve respect, even if it means disagreeing with the person or calling him to account for some action.[7] Totally ignoring someone in our sphere of attention—except in crowds—

would be disrespectful, in fact a type of microaggression, and would show negative prejudice.

Honneth's third sphere of recognition, acknowledging the positive qualities in a person, relates to another discussion by Maclagan on respect for persons as a moral principle. In a second article (1960, 289–305), on the practical meaning of that principle, he considers what guidance the principle provides for our lives. Taking the teleological position in ethics—what ends we attempt to achieve with our conduct—he identifies two such different ends or goals toward which we direct our actions: "the relief of misery and the increase of happiness," and "the realization of values." Achieving happiness is not sufficient by itself because the worth and dignity of human life requires not just what is likeable but what is admirable. The principle of respect functions to set limits within which we must pursue our ends (1960, 290–91).

Maclagan continues by observing that while it is quite natural to pursue our own happiness, a concern for others' happiness is a moral concern. Achieving even just this one goal requires a certain kind of respect that Maclagan says needs to be given to animals as well (1960, 292) since they too have the capacity for happiness or unhappiness (pleasure or pain). But "there is an appropriate attitude toward persons which can be adopted only toward persons," and "that relates to our concern for values rather than our concern for their happiness" (1960, 293). Thus the other end or goal, the realization of values, is a specifically human concern. Our attitude toward other humans

> must also be governed by the recognition that as persons they, like ourselves, have not only a natural interest in their own happiness but a moral interest in values, and thus in the dignity of life. Furthermore, this latter interest, precisely because values are values and it *is* a moral interest, must by them as by us be accorded a general priority. How, after all, could we more grossly insult our fellows than by implying, in our treatment of them, that while *we* indeed have such an interest *they* do not. (Maclagan 1960, 293, emphasis his)

Maclagan's discussion implies that both of these ends—the pursuit of happiness and the realization of values—require us to make others' ends our own. The one concerned with values, however, has a deeper meaning: we must make sure that our actions do not take away the others' initiative. We must appreciate the others' efforts to realize their values, such as competence, self-sufficiency, or kindness. Even when assistance is required, we must encourage the recipients of help to be co-agents rather than mere beneficiaries of our actions. That insures their dignity. These "others, like ourselves, are essentially *agents*" (Maclagan 1960, 295, his emphasis); to deny that is to insult their dignity. Habitat for Humanity provides a good example of being mindful of this by requiring that the recipients of a house participate in the building process.

Recognition in this case means acknowledging the good qualities of the other person, not assuming oneself to be the sole possessor of these qualities. Respect requires such recognition and it acknowledges the other as an agent. Mistakes in that arena are sometimes made in various contexts, such as research with human subjects, medical work, charity work or other "do-goodism." Professional ethical guidelines (e.g., Belmont Report 1979) have been developed and are constantly updated to guard against that problem in research and human services. In my research on religious charity, mentioned in previous chapters, respondents were asked how they felt about the word "charity." One woman from a Lutheran Church left no doubt about it. "*I hate it!*" she declared, emphatically, explaining what it connotes: "I'm better than you're, so poor dear I'll help you." She preferred words like "caring" and "sharing." Her pastor also felt that charity implies downgrading the recipient (Terian 1984, 304). The problem with "do-goodism" is condescension that implies hierarchical thinking, and that may be a threat to the self-esteem of the recipient. On the other hand, "*autonomy-oriented help* consists of giving recipients assistance in the form of tools they can use to solve the problem on their own" (Nadler et al. 2010, 186, emphasis theirs). That is an example of both recognition and respect, and assuming that the person we don't know is a competent agent is positive prejudice.

Continuing in Honneth's third sphere, communal recognition, it should be noted that such recognition is also due to people who may not have notable achievements or other valued qualities that usually warrant recognition. Giselsson discusses why a "cognitively damaged" girl, Sesha, should be respected: "because she belongs to a human community, and, as a human, is born into a structure of communal being and moral significance that differs from animal being" (2012, 164). Thus she is recognized as a unique individual, a member of the community in which others make up for her deficiencies, and in which she is valued regardless of her abilities. This is a miniature picture of what community—even society—is all about because no one is self-sufficient in all aspects of life.

Honneth (2012, 85) considers recognition "a moral act" because it involves a "restriction of egocentrism." Although elsewhere he states that the relation of recognition to the Kantian concept of respect remains unclear (Honneth 2012, 79), here he makes the connection in the moral sphere. Referring to Kant's (1964) discussion of respect, he observes that Kant's "conception of worth compels us to impose a restriction on our actions which 'thwarts' our 'self-love.'" Building on Kant, Honneth goes even further: "to recognize others is to perceive an evaluative quality in them that motivates us intrinsically to behave no longer egocentrically, but rather in accordance with the intentions, desires and needs of others" (Honneth 2012, 85). Levinas would agree, as discussed earlier in this book. To achieve such a state of mind, Honneth observes that it is a "learning process" and should become part of the life-world, in fact a "second nature" (2012, 82, 85). In an earlier work, Honneth (1996, 175) discusses Hegel and Mead who both visualize "the same ideal of a society in which the universalistic achievements of equality and individualism would be so embedded in patterns of interaction that all subjects would be recognized as both autonomous and individuated, equal and particular persons." In such an ideal society, respect would be widespread.

Sometimes, however, recognition is used as an ideological tool for domination, something that the Marxist scholar Louis Althusser (2001) wrote about. Honneth (2012, 75–97) discusses this at length, showing that "ritual" or symbolic affirmations—such as calling employees "creative entrepreneurs" or praising today's woman "for her virtues as a good housewife," fail to reinforce these persons' self-worth (2012, 91, 87). Similarly, emotional appeals and false compliments have the opposite effect of true recognition in that they "fail to promote personal autonomy" (2012, 76). Recognition must "apply to abilities and virtues that the addressees really do possess" (2012, 87) and that they value; that is, recognition must be credible to the addressee. Furthermore, recognition must take tangible forms, such as material fulfillment or other real acknowledgment of the person's true value. Reiterating that "recognition represents a moral act anchored in the social world as an everyday occurrence," Honneth provides four premises for true recognition: (1) As the German usage of the term means, it is "the affirmation of positive qualities of human subjects or groups"; (2) it is "an attitude realized in concrete action"; (3) it must be "explicitly intended"; and (4) its "sub-species" are the three spheres of love, legal respect, and esteem (2012, 80). Respect is present in all of these, thus respect and recognition are two sides of the same coin, positive prejudice underlying both.

MUTUALITY IN RESPECT

It is obvious that respect cannot be one-directional, that mutuality is implied in true respect. Recognizing that helps solve the other problem Green (2010, 214) worried about, that of "containing" the rule of respect for persons. When everyone demands respect, he asks, "is there any decent way to avoid respect inflation . . . ?" The thought itself is somewhat absurd. It seems obvious that respect is a quality that has no limits—the more the better. At the bottom of this worry appears to be an idea that respect should be given only to a few privileged people, that the masses should not expect to be respected. This thought runs counter to the concept of respect, discussed above, as due to every human being simply by virtue of being human. Furthermore, it seems inconceivable that such universal respect would somehow cheapen it. On the contrary, if everyone were to give and demand respect, this would create an ideal society.

Mutual respect begins with self-respect. Even for Kant, self-esteem was a duty; "not respecting ourselves is immoral," and "a person who disrespects himself is not capable to fulfill the duties he has towards others" (Lawrence-Lightfoot 1999, 44, referring to Kant). But self-respect comes from being respected by others; dignity comes from being recognized as a member of a community (Honneth 1996, 79, referring to Mead). These are communal products, and the production flows both ways: genuine concern for others' welfare and personhood enhances our own personhood as well as theirs. As Christian Smith (2010, 406–8) describes it, it is a "team sport." Self-respect and respect for others thus mutually reinforce each other, and both depend on relationships. "The more we interpret external signs about our person in the light of human dignity and develop an *assured* self-esteem the more we are ready to pay respect to the worthiness of our fellow human beings" (Lawrence-Lightfoot 1999, 51, emphasis hers).

So that is the ideal. But how are we to deal with people who do not respect others? In an interesting article on the rudeness of some airport officials and store clerks, a British novelist, Rachel Cusk (2017), describes her male companion's exemplary behavior. He kept his calm, looked at the airport official in the eyes and asked for her advice. She comments that he had both self-respect and respect for the woman, and implicitly criticizes the phony friendliness of a clothing store customer service person. Furthermore, it helps to remember that the rude person may be having a hard day. When Brené Brown (2015, 107–16) observed a disrespectful customer at a bank, she thought, generously: "people generally do the best they can." She kept asking other people what they thought about that idea until she came to believe in it herself. Yet she emphasizes that people are to be held accountable. Respect requires that, as discussed above. Positive prejudice would attribute others' rudeness to their having an unusually bad day, not taking it personally but adopting a forgiving spirit, keeping one's own calm and self-respect. Such attitude usually calms the other person down as well.

This, however, is not always easy when one experiences frequent micro-aggressions. While critiques label microaggressions as examples of victim-hood culture (e.g., Friedersdorf 2015; Campbell and Manning 2018) that promote psychological fragility and prevent free speech, the experience of those at the receiving end testifies to the harmful effects of such interactions. Even deciding how to respond can be stressful. A healthy response involves mutuality. In his short article, Nadal (2014) summarizes extensive research on this topic by Sue and his team, and others. He notes that it is a "Catch 22"; responding may bring about "arguments, defensiveness, denials, or additional microaggressions" (e.g., "I was just joking"), but not responding can lead to "regret, resentment, and sadness." Responses can be either passive-aggressive (e.g., rolling one's eyes), proactive (maybe yell back), or assertive, which means to calmly tell the Other how the comment made you feel, and perhaps grasp the opportunity to educate the person. And the "guilty" one does best to own up and apologize, which would bring mutual respect back to the interchange. In any case, it is important for a minority person who frequently experiences microaggressions to seek support of loved ones and others with similar experiences (Nadal 2014, 71–74). One's hurts and self-image can heal in the company of supportive and respecting others.

Mutuality and self-respect, moreover, are tested in situations in which people have against their will been made subservient to others. "In the vice of servility," Lawrence-Lightfoot (1999, 46) writes, "an individual demonstrates a lack of self-respect; as a reasoned being one has the duty to treat his own self as an end, and not put this self as means to the disposal of another person in the sense of servility."[8] It is a good point, but at the same time it can be seen as blaming the victim. In many cases exercising autonomy is physically impossible, or the price is too high—think of some Saudi women running away from home at the risk of their lives, or whole families becoming refugees, leaving everything behind![9] Another situation is what Karl Marx would call false consciousness, taking one's subservience as normal. Referring to Frantz Fanon (1967), Giselsson (2012, 62) writes: "those who are subjugated often suffer from internal colonization, a self-hatred that makes the insistence of one's worth and respect for one's wishes difficult."

Kant and other philosophers behind the universal principle of respect did not visualize such problems in their emphasis on treating others as ends in themselves, and putting others above oneself. As several writers, such as Giselsson (2012), Dorothy Smith (2010), and others have observed, their idea comes from the viewpoint of privileged white European males. The noble exhortations to prioritize the other sound too much like the familiar state of things to oppressed people who are "being given over in slavery and servitude to the other" (Giselsson 2012, 47). And Giselsson continues: "But if we were to place an actual slave, or a woman in the place of the Ego, such unconditional giving and prioritization of the other looks, frighteningly, like the all-too-familiar roles expected of women and the subjugated: subordinate yourself to the demand of others, sacrifice all for an other whose needs are always more important."

"What women were denied," Giselsson (2012, 191) explains, "was the possibility of *reciprocal* accountability, that they could hold others to account over injuries done to them" (her emphasis). Thus, important as self-respect is, it is hard to conjure up when the person does not get respect from others. The "struggle" for recognition that Hegel wrote about is historically correct as recognition and respect for oppressed groups has usually come only after intense, collective struggles, such as demonstrations, strikes, social movements and other large-scale demands. And the fact that these demands take place is *"one* example of the presence of both the expectation of accountability and the existence of a communal standard" (Giselsson 2012, 203, emphasis hers) which "assumes moral equality" (2012, 200). Our acknowledgment of the rightness of such campaigns, furthermore, shows the general acceptance of mutual accountability in our human endeavors and thus the dignity and moral worth of each human being and their communities.

There are several more benign interpersonal attitudes and approaches that run counter to mutual respect. For example, a lack of reciprocal accountability can degenerate into paternalism (Giselsson 2012, 205), even with kindest intentions but with negative results to the addressee's self-respect. Condescension is another attitude that used to be viewed positively within a hierarchical social structure but in professedly egalitarian societies implies looking down on the other and thus rules out mutual respect. Even compassion—"without fellow feeling and love for our fellow humans"—"makes for an unstable foundation for respect" (Giselsson 2012, 171). To give further examples, one-upmanship is a form of superiority, sanctimonious behavior is all about oneself, and one giving false promises is not herself accountable. Objectification, as I have observed earlier, makes the other person a "thing" and therefore precludes respect due to humans. Sexualization has historically been done to women and sadly, it continues to this day, objectifying women and using them for some men's own ends. Microaggressions is another name for some of these behaviors, as discussed above. Over time, these can lead to serious effects, such as "lack of confidence, low self-esteem, depression, anxiety and self-hatred, all of which can lead to self-harm and suicide" (Giselsson 2012, 180, footnote 58).

Mutuality in respect is therefore essential. Clients generally respect competent professionals to whom they have gone for help or advice, but sometimes respect doesn't flow the other way. Lawrence-Lightfoot (1999) interviewed several professionals who exemplified respect toward their clients and associates. For example, a medical doctor, Johnye Ballenger, made an extra effort to develop relationships with her patients to counteract the legacy of her medical school that "has probably exaggerated their paternalism, their elitism, and their dogma." She discovered that sometimes "respect was expressed through *doing very little* when there is little to do," but "simply being present, attentive, and loving" (Lawrence-Lightfoot 1999, 84, 88, emphasis hers). An interview with Harvard law professor David Wilkins brought out another dimension of respect: making oneself vulnerable, which is "an act of trust and respect." In Wilkins's words: "You can't show respect for someone else unless you are prepared to make yourself vulnerable. You can't give respect unless you have the courage to say what you need from the other person" (Lawrence-Lightfoot 1999, 194). And an Episcopal priest and pastoral psychotherapist, Bill Wallace, "believes that the quality of *attention* is the most important dimension of respectful relationships," relating "to the 'essence' of who he or she is as a person." In Wallace's words, for respectful demeanor "you somehow need to reveal that you too struggle with some of these issues" (Lawrence-Lightfoot 1999, 198, 222, emphasis hers). All these examples show the professionals' respect toward their clients; they did not put themselves on a pedestal but met the clients at the human level.

The philosopher John Lachs (2014) gives another interesting idea on respect. In his little, thought provoking book, *Meddling*, he advocates individualism and promotes the ethics of freedom: leaving people alone, letting them do as they please as long as it doesn't hurt anyone else. "Respect for others consists primarily in acknowledging them as worthy decision makers," he writes, or "as autonomous self-determining agents." He compares violations of one's autonomy almost to "minor forms of death, . . . as every event of meddling breaks off the intimate connection between decision and enactment, rendering people incapacitated or inactive" (2014, 37, 46). Regarding helping, he says: "To give true help is to become an instrument of the other's will, honoring the integrity of what the needy want instead of telling them what they ought to have" (2014, 10). In fact, psychological testing has shown a weak or no correlation between helpfulness and nurturance but a pretty strong correlation of helpfulness with dominance or assertiveness (Penner and Orom 2010, 62). Even in the area of communication, Lachs's advice is "to say little and to say it cautiously at the start, and watch for interest and willingness to hear more" (2014, 59).[10] The best approach to others is "to cheer them on," to "serve as a midwife to self-discovery" (2014, 73, 105–6). Such approach, individualistic as it may be, nevertheless supports the communal idea of mutual respect. It is also positive prejudice because it assumes that the other is competent.

POSITIVE PREJUDICE AS RESPECT FOR DIFFERENCE

To bring the discussion back to prejudice and its relation to respect, I need to address the meaning of universalism and particularism. As mentioned above in the discussion on Maclagan's (1960) article, universalism—the Enlightenment philosophy—implies impartiality, which is rational and ethical at some levels but falls short of the requirement of respect for persons. Particularism, attention to and appreciation of the unique qualities of individual persons and groups, is needed to really show respect to them. With its individualism, universalism accomplished some good things like attention to human rights with its emphasis on the equality of all human beings. Criticism of that philosophy that I have mentioned a few times earlier, however, is based on the fact that the wisdom of the time did not conceive universalism as comprehensively as we understand it today. Thus women, racial or sexual minorities, laborers, the poor, servant classes, and people in colonized countries were left out of the call for "universal" human rights. In a true sense, then, Enlightenment did not live up to its own ethic in that it was particularistic in its white male European orientation.

Some kind of new particularism was needed to direct attention to these neglected groups of people. A whole school of "post-humanist" writers—for example, Lyotard (e.g., 1984), Derrida (e.g., 1973), Foucault (e.g., 1971), and the critical theorists Adorno and Horkheimer (Tarr 2011) mentioned in chapter 3—criticized universalism on the grounds that it did not give respect to all. These writers did not, however, offer any "grounds as to *why* difference should be respected," so ultimately their theories too rest on "humanist and universalist assumptions" (Giselsson 2012, 105–6, emphasis hers). The above-mentioned campaigns by workers, racial and ethnic minorities, women, sexual minorities, the differentially abled, and others have brought attention to their *particular* needs and that they, too, with their own specific identities, need to be counted in the universal human rights endeavor. That has expanded the understanding so that now most everyone agrees that universalism must count all humans in. In the racial sphere, that brought about the idea of color-blindness, that everyone should have equal rights regardless of the color of their skin. In that manner, organizations now declare that they do not discriminate based on race, religion, disability, sex or sexual orientation, etc. This all sounds good, but something was still missing from the equation.

Throwing everyone in the same pool of humanity ignored many things. For one thing, it ignored the unequal history of these groups. Giving equal rights to people with such different starting points still leaves glaring inequalities unaddressed. Affirmative action and programs like busing to integrate schools were designed to address that problem for racial minorities, but these programs had their problems too. Aside from these, there was another problem with being melted in the one huge pool of humanity: it ignored difference and therefore resulted in lost identity with its accompanying loss of self-esteem. The concrete circumstances of different groups and their identities needed special attention; members of these groups needed recognition for who they were, their unique identities, histories, cultures, characteristics, and struggles. Universalism looked at everything from the white European male standpoint, and that resulted in neglect of the special human qualities of other people and groups. In spite of good intentions, negative prejudice was there because being different implicitly meant being a problem.

As explained in chapter 3, prejudice is an attitude toward people or groups that are different in some respects from the majority. The point here is that universalism ignored difference, or at least did not provide sufficient justification for respecting difference, as Giselsson (2012, 2) observes. Deviation from the norm implied a problem. This underlying assumption had ramifications for everyday life in a multicultural society. For one example, Lachs (2014, 82) writes that "we distrust people with foreign accents [and] avoid those who voice strange desires." And those who look different are often inadvertently left out of informal, spontaneous interactions. Drawing too small a circle is how negative prejudice works, as observed in chapter 3, and that is obviously not respectful. Developing an attitude of positive prejudice that recognizes and respects those who are different and appreciates their positive qualities is a learning process, as Honneth (2012, 82, 85) explains, until it becomes a second nature. "Respect is not something one can imitate," Lawrence-Lightfoot (1999, 57) asserts, "but something one must embody," and it is expressed and maintained by respectful acts. Maclagan's (1960) explanation of sympathy makes the same point: passive human sympathy is prerequisite to the active kind, but neither one can exist without the other.

Being measured by an improper yardstick renders one inadequate; there is a foreign element in the equation. "The people who must believe they are white can never be your measuring stick," Coates (2015, 108) advises his son. For a true interpersonal encounter, no "means" should interfere: "Every means is an obstacle. Only where all means have disintegrated encounters occur" (Buber 1970, 63). Foreign criteria can be such means because they prevent seeing the person in his own right. Other examples of such "means" would include using the other for one's own purposes, as a "bridge" to something else, or even to satisfy one's curiosity. This would preclude focusing on the other person for his own sake. While we may not know much about the other person, we know that he is a fellow human being and thus a subject; to understand him "demands sympathy or love, ways of being that are different from impassive contemplation" (Levinas 1998, 5). Furthermore, he has his own unique qualities and therefore is not merely another specimen of humanity. Ethical responsibility toward him implies first acknowledging that. The universalistic idea of color-blindness errs in that respect; it fails to meet the other with that person's unique qualities, history, and circumstances. It does not honor difference.

Yet, it is universalism correctly understood that gives justification for respecting those who are different. Giselsson (2012, 83–84) "suggests" that "claims for particularism and universalism are mutually dependent rather than mutually exclusive, and that some form of universalism needs to be retained in order to justify respect for difference." In other words, universalism provides the ground for particularism, but then one must acknowledge the different plants that grow on the ground. It is the "universal conception of worth" that guarantees the respect, but that must include acceptance of the variety of human types, experiences, and goals. Such variety must be accepted within communities as well, which again brings about the idea of individual rights. Giselsson (2012, 106) summarizes this as follows: "It is in this sense that universal humanism is necessarily dependent on particularism, in that in order to warrant its functions as a representation of humanity it must necessarily reflect the heterogeneous nature of humanity, while at the same time reflecting that we are in some way the *same*" (emphasis Giselsson's).

The fact that in "some way" we all are the same is the "shared horizon" that Gadamer wrote about, as reviewed in chapter 3. Existentially that is even more than "some way"; Christakis's (2019, 408) biological data—that at least 99 percent of the DNA in all humans is *exactly* the same—implies that almost all basic life concerns for all humans are the same. As the human "shared horizon," this should enable us to understand others and help us draw a wider, more inclusive circle. It must not, however, blind us to human differences that are integral parts of their identities. Persons can best grow to their potential in communities "within which distinctiveness and diversity are not only tolerated but also, for the sake of personal flourishing, nurtured and celebrated" (Christian Smith 2010, 404). Prejudice, then, as the lens through which we see the world, must provide a wide enough vision that includes all, and a clear enough vision to see human beings in their historical circumstances and specific identities, to see their true value in this infinite variety, and to see this variety as a positive feature.

CONCLUSION

Respect or the lack of it shows in our everyday interactions, as my initial example of my own interaction with the basket-weaving lady illustrates. Human dignity is a real, ontological feature that separates humans from the rest of the natural world. The philosophical justification for why people need to be respected was most clearly given by the Enlightenment philosopher Immanuel Kant who stipulated that each person should "treat himself and all others" as ends and not as mere means, simply because we are persons. The philosopher Maclagan analyzed this maxim and concluded that true respect requires not only a duty felt by the rational will but also a "natural factor" which is our capacity for sympathy (really meaning what many others call empathy). Kant's idea has been criticized as not providing a sufficient foundation for respect, which Honneth sees as "human self-realization" and Giselsson as "reciprocal accountability." Recognition is part of such respect, and my claim is that positive prejudice underlies it.

Respect also requires mutuality. That means self-respect must be its foundation that then enables the person to demand respect and to give it to others. The Enlightenment philosophers came from a white, male, privileged European background and therefore did not visualize their universalism as including marginalized groups, such as women, ethnic and other minorities, and the colonized. Their rights have been achieved by collective "struggles," though full equality is still to be achieved. The fact that the marginalized groups have demanded respect and that we recognize the rightness of these demands shows that there is a universal standard to be achieved, while particularism is needed to include those who are different. Respect, then, goes beyond equal rights. It must include subtle everyday interactions that recognize the identities and unique characteristics and circumstances of people and groups. The fact that we don't know enough about most people and groups calls for positive prejudice in our approach to them.

NOTES

1. Giselsson credits the concept of accountability to Stephen Darwall (2006).
2. Christakis (2019, 397) disagrees with the premise of human specialness. To him, "humans are not so special," but he argues, "our closeness to animals actually reveals our common humanity."
3. Smith (2010, 99, footnote 13) states: "Personalism has strong affinities with theism, although that connection is not necessary." And he goes on to cite atheistic and pantheistic versions of personalism (see Burrow 1999). And Giselsson (2012, 170–171) discusses "a need for theories of moral consideration that do not actively exclude—but do not necessarily rely on—the possibility of the divine, as such theories would be more inclusive and reflective of the actual diversity of human belief systems."
4. As discussed in chapter 1, romantic love can also become possessive and thus objectify the loved one, making her a thing.
5. This happens in human crowds as well and is sometimes called social contagion.
6. As discussed above, according to the philosophy of personalism the special ontological nature of human dignity provides a reason why human ends are to be respected.
7. It is for this reason that Maclagan (1960, 301) is opposed to the medicalization of deviance in that it "amounts to a denial of personal responsibility" and thus "*insults* the wrongdoer under the guise of *safeguarding* his interests." He asserts, "a man has a *right* to be punished" (emphasis his). Also, Honneth (1996, 53) shows that for Hegel the lack of recognition was the motive for crime.
8. Lawrence-Lightfoot here has a reference to Hill (1973).
9. *"Even rational individuals often cannot successfully hold other rational individuals accountable over injuries and wrongs, which is precisely why Western societies have communal law enforcement"* (Giselsson 2012, 190, emphasis hers). But the situation can feel almost hopeless when there is no law protecting the oppressed.
10. The reader may recall from chapter 2 similar advice given by Shannon Sullivan (1997) that she called "hypothetical construction," offering one's ideas as something to be worked on together.

Chapter Five

Ethical Prejudice

In light of the foregoing chapters, it seems evident that prejudice is not something we can eliminate or avoid but is the very basis for perception and understanding. The difference lies in the kind of prejudice (prejudgment) that we manifest in our interactions. I have tried to put the concept in a larger perspective by providing the context and background in which our interactions take place and in which the kind of prejudice makes a difference. Chapter 1 showed the importance of others and their attitudes by explaining how the formation and maintenance of self depends on feedback and support from others. Phenomenology helps us understand how we experience our interactions, and these experiences make a world of difference in our self-esteem, emotions, and motivations—in our very ability to be the best we can be. Ethical approach toward other people is to enhance their well-being by seeing them as subjects with agency and their own goals, supporting them to become their best selves.

The second chapter examined interpersonal encounters in which the above-mentioned dynamics come to the fore. Different contexts of the interacting parties, such as their cultural, historical, and personal backgrounds, present challenges to understanding and can lead to different definitions of situations. While shared symbols make interaction possible, acknowledging the ultimate difference of the other person—accompanied by an open, hypothetical attitude and willingness to negotiate—leads to a positive definition of the situation in which both parties can feel affirmed and empowered. The effects of each encounter lead to consequences that either help or hinder personal development. Close relationships are also built of separate encounters that then have a cumulative effect, thus some of the same dynamics are present in them as in encounters between strangers.

Chapter 3 delved specifically into the concept of prejudice as a general prejudgment, tracing its history and changing meanings. We cannot get rid of emotions, expectations, and prior orientations based on our previous knowledge or hunch; on the contrary, these make perception possible, and we understand from our life circumstance. Are we then doomed to look down on all others who are in some way different from us? As I tried to explain, the answer lies in the different types of prejudice. Positive prejudice acknowledges that we belong to the same human family with other people and groups, however different they may be. We share the same horizons and therefore can identify with these others as our kind of species. Furthermore, with humility we realize that our knowledge and previous hunches are always inadequate and may be entirely wrong and therefore in need of correction. By drawing a larger circle and employing the better angels of our nature we can make positive prejudice the norm. Not only "innocent until proven guilty" but also valuable in their own right should be our characterization of other people. That is positive prejudice and an ethical approach toward other people.

Chapter 4 then dealt with the concept of respect that is at the heart of positive prejudice. Human dignity is an ontological given, thus humans are to be respected, period. This means that each person is to be treated as an end and not merely as a means. It means mutual respect, both giving and receiving respect, apologizing when brought to account about disrespectful behavior, and respecting oneself as a foundation for respecting others. Recognition in a community is a basic human need, often resulting in a struggle by marginalized groups—such as women, ethnic and other minorities, and the colonized—that have not received adequate recognition. Because there is a universal standard of justice, we acknowledge the rightness of such struggles. Yet there is need for particularism that acknowledges difference and recognizes the unique histories, identities, and needs of other individuals and groups.

In this concluding chapter, my aim is to look at prejudice and respect in a somewhat different light and thus reconsider their meaning in everyday life. With examples, I endeavor to show what positive prejudice means in our interactions, its relation to trust, what difference it makes for a person at the receiving end, and when caution in our relationships is in order. Most of us experience multiple interpersonal encounters each day. While our individualistic culture holds each person responsible for their own feelings and motivations, it is much easier to believe in yourself and work toward your goals and personal improvement when others give signals that they believe in you. Experiencing positive prejudice empowers a person; ethics requires giving that to others. Thus there is such a thing as ethical prejudice.

PREJUDICE AS A TENDENCY TO FILL IN THE GAP

While prejudice—a prejudgment or preconceived idea—is always present in our interpersonal encounters, it is more so when we don't know the other very well. Let us begin with a hypothetical example. You board an airplane and find your seat next to some stranger. Since all perception is based on generalities first, the Other is merely an object of your initial perception; the seat next to you is occupied, so you don't put your bag on it. But since that object is a human being, you now confront "a consciousness seen from the outside, the paradox of a thought that resides in the exterior" (Merleau-Ponty 2012, 364). That other human being is like you but she is not you; she is a mystery to you. As discussed in chapter 2, the macro-level cultural and institutional context provides the structure and norms to the encounter, and at the meso-level you place this person in some of the categorical units—such as gender and approximate age, examples of the generalities. But you most likely know nothing about the other generalities, such as the corporate units this person represents. And when it comes to particularities, such as her micro-level relationships, experiences, background, aims, and feelings, you know nothing. Yet these factors make a difference in how she sees the world, and a relationship is created between you and her whether you want it or not. You may acknowledge the relationship by greeting her when you first meet.

What happens next depends on your cultural norms and the signals you read from the Other's behavior. How would someone with positive prejudice proceed? You may have already begun by greeting her and thus acknowledging her humanness. In any case, you belong to the same human family and share the same situation on the airplane. Yet a wide gap exists in your knowledge of one another. If you are in the mood for socializing and thus interested in filling the gap accurately, you watch for signals. These days most people sitting on a plane are either reading, working on their computers, or have their earphones on listening to music or watching a movie. In that case respect probably means leaving them alone, unless interruption becomes necessary for some reason. But if we go back years or decades to a time when people still often talked with their seatmate, the Other may also appear open to communication. In today's America it doesn't seem right to ask at the outset, "What do you do for a living?" That would seem like interrogation or at least invasion of privacy. So perhaps you make a remark about the weather, or the crowded plane, or the delayed departure—types of phatic communication that can take place comfortably and naturally. If the Other responds and makes related comments herself, you may find a companion for the flight and gradually fill in some of the gap with true information. The point is, however, that positive prejudice respects the distance and does not try to fill in the gap if the Other seems uninterested.

Racial profiling is an example of a hasty urge to fill in the gap with our guessing when we don't know the Other. A retired Major League Baseball player, Doug Glanville (2014), describes one such incident that happened to him. On a winter day in Hartford, Connecticut, he was shoveling his driveway when a police officer from the predominantly white next town, West Hartford, stopped, walked to him and remarked: "So, you trying to make a few extra bucks, shoveling people's driveways around here?" With great restraint at this microaggression, Mr. Glanville explained that this was his house, and the police left without an apology. Eventually Mr. Glanville made it a teachable moment by going to the West Hartford police department to discuss the incident. It turned out that the police officer was looking for a man who had broken West Hartford's ordinance against door-to-door solicitation. Nevertheless, there was no excuse for assuming guilt based on race. Other people in the neighborhood were shoveling their driveways too but did not get such disturbing visits. Racial profiling sometimes serves as a shortcut, but no shortcut is appropriate when human beings and their lives are at stake.

Properly meeting another person means accepting him as a mystery. But this mystery is not like a sunset that we merely admire—another human being is not a phenomenon[1] like a sunset; this mystery is a human being, thus dealing with him demands a relationship. This does not, however, call for the false friendliness that is sometimes exhibited by service personnel or salespeople. A car salesman may invite the customer to his office and even show pictures of his family (as happened to me and my husband more than once), or a vacuum-cleaner salesman may enter your home and act like a long-lost friend. Such artificial warmth and closeness may even seem comical, and it is disrespectful because it is fake. Although kindness and friendliness are important cultural values, as is the need to respect the stranger, ethics does not require blurring the line between friends and strangers. In his *Principles of Social Justice*, Miller (1999) divides relationships into three types, one based on a social bond (family), another on desert (business), and the third on equality (citizenship). Accepting the relationship at its proper level as a business relationship is respectful, and the citizenship level implies respect in a more distant manner, as I have suggested. All in all, respect toward the stranger is accepting the distance and not assuming that this stranger is like oneself. Yet, as Kant's philosophy asserts, respect means not treating the person merely as a means but at the same time as an end in himself (see chapter 4).

Here I acknowledge my Northern European cultural bias. As I was growing up in ancient Finland, we were not expected to greet strangers on country roads. As a little girl, I was expected to curtsy to people I knew but ignore those I didn't know. In most rural American settings that may seem rude, but there the distance between strangers and acquaintances was acknowledged.

The fact that there was no expectation of familiarity with a stranger didn't mean disrespect, just an acknowledgment that strangers were not part of our immediate world. Strangers, however, were respected in a somewhat distant kind of way. This was exemplified by the fact that if one addressed a stranger one would use a formal form of address, including the plural form of you. I still remember feeling so grown-up when I was fifteen and someone addressed me in the formal way. In some other parts of the world strangers have been viewed with suspicion,[2] but what I am referring to did not involve suspicion, just an acknowledgment of the distance. In America the line may sometimes be blurred; the norm of general friendliness may lead to undue familiarity with strangers. Familiarity and respect do not necessarily mean the same.

This does not mean that one cultural norm is better than another. Each culture has its advantages and disadvantages; maintaining distance may seem too cold for comfort, and using titles and the plural form of you makes interactions stiff and formal, but too much warmth and closeness may make one gullible. Indeed, sometimes familiarity with strangers can backfire. Gladwell (2019) provides multiple examples when caution would have resulted in a better outcome. Greater openness brings greater vulnerability to the interaction in that the Other might take advantage of one's openness and friendliness. As noted above, respect and positive prejudice need not mean the same openness toward strangers as one has toward close friends with whom one has a close social bond. Personal relationships and business relationships thus need not be mixed up or thrown in the same pool; blurring the line between them can lead to the blind trust that crooks can take advantage of. One can respect a stranger without undue trust and its accompanying vulnerability.

When we meet an acquaintance or a friend the gap in our knowledge of the Other still exists, though it is smaller—the closer the relationship the narrower the gap. Moreover, in that case we are more apt to engage in a conversation that will help fill in the gap. We can direct our attention and remarks to areas that we know are of interest to the other person. When the person next to us on the airplane happens to be an old acquaintance or friend, we have no problem socializing. But even in closer relationships it often happens that we think we know more about the Other than we actually do. That can easily lead to stereotyping, taking the Other for granted, trusting the person too much (Gladwell 2019), and other such mistakes that lead us to forget that the Other is a mystery to us. To use "hypothetical construction" (see chapter 2) in communication means to respect that otherness and tread softly at the presence of the mystery, accepting that our ideas are only hypotheses, colored by our own backgrounds and prejudices, and then working together toward a more objective truth.

Our own life situation is thus the other part of the context of all interpersonal encounters. We have a "situated understanding," as Sandel (2014, 210–11) explains. Our life situation tends to lead us to filling in the gap with material that we are familiar with, what seems correct. You have met an Asian who is a computer whiz and conclude that all Asians are smart with computers. Such false generalization is stereotyping and needs correction; if we are willing to listen, the Other may eventually offer some detail about her life that helps us fill in some of the gap. "Getting to know someone . . . [we] can bring ourselves within his or her perspective" (Sandel 2014, 99). When that is not possible, however, positive prejudice calls us to refrain from generalizations and respect the distance. As observed earlier, the first step in ethical encounters is to be aware of the gap, to acknowledge it to oneself. Such acknowledgment avoids negative prejudice. My claim is that acknowledging the gap, giving the other the benefit not of the doubt but of the status of a stranger or of a person we don't know well enough, and assuming that the person has good qualities that we don't know, is positive prejudice. Negative prejudice is not the gap in our understanding; rather, it is the hunch, the material from our "stock of knowledge" (Schutz) with which we tend to generalize to fill in the gap. Avoiding such generalization is the beginning of a positive attitude.

In short, prejudice is the attitude we tend to form on the basis of our sketchy, flimsy ideas about the Other, especially when we try to fill in the gap with our "knowledge." Even when the "knowledge" about the Other's categorical unit—such as his ethnic group—is positive, it may be stereotypical and not true of this particular person whose strength may be in something else. Thus it does not respect the individuality of the Other. When we cannot accurately fill in the gap, positive prejudice accepts the distance and respects the stranger in the status of a stranger who nevertheless is most likely a good person, at any rate has his own interests and goals in life. Awareness is the first step toward correction; when we catch ourselves generalizing from our sketchy knowledge or hunch and stop the process, we are on the way to positive prejudice. We can then draw a larger circle that includes the other person as part of "us." That leads us to value him as a member of our own species with whom we share the human horizon. In spite of the fact that we don't know him well or at all, we appreciate who he is and what he brings to this world that we share.

TRUST AND POSITIVE PREJUDICE

Some type or level of trust is involved in all interpersonal association. We develop this basic trust in infancy as our needs are met by loving others (Erikson 1963; Honneth 1996). At the very basic level, trust is "an attitude of positive expectation about other people, a sense that they are basically well intentioned and unlikely to harm us" (Govier 1998, 6). Without such basic trust social life would not be possible. According to the sociologist Simmel, "without the general trust that people have in each other, society itself would disintegrate, for very few relationships are based entirely upon what is known with certainty about another person, and very few relationships would endure if trust were not as strong as, or stronger than, rational proof or personal observation" (1907/1978, 178–179).

Trust includes cognitive, emotional, and behavioral dimensions (Lewis and Weigert 1985; Borum 2010). All these components are present in trust but in different proportions and at different levels. For one cognitive example of a basic level trust, when we pass another person on a sidewalk we expect that person to mind her own business and not bother us. Because of racism that is still too prevalent in our society, however, some groups in the population do not enjoy such basic trust. Coates writes to his son: "You have been cast into a race in which the wind is always at your face and the hounds are always at your heels" (2015, 107). And he tells of his own experience of uneasiness in a public place, compared to white people:

> I saw white parents pushing double-wide strollers down gentrifying Harlem boulevards in T-shirts and jogging shorts . . . or in conversation . . . while their sons commanded entire sidewalks with their tricycles. The galaxy belonged to them, and as terror was communicated to our children, I saw mastery communicated to theirs. And so when I remember pushing you in your stroller to other parts of the city, the West Village for instance, almost instinctively believing that you should see more, I remember feeling ill at ease, like I had borrowed someone else's heirloom, like I was travelling under an assumed name. (Coates 2015, 89)

Obviously, basic trust was shaky at best in this case, leading to negative emotions. Trust was shaken even more in another incident: at one time, when Coates's four-year-old son was slow in getting out of an elevator, a white woman pushed him, saying "Come on!" A stranger "invoked their right over the body of my son," he writes, and this act angered him greatly (2015, 94). Obviously, such examples of negative prejudice erode trust and make life in public challenging.

Yet we need at least some level of trust if we are to manage our lives in public. As on the sidewalks or in elevators, we have the same expectation toward other passengers on the plane or bus that we are on, that we can travel in peace. We also trust that the air captain or bus driver will do her best to take us safely to our destination. Gladwell states that in our relationships with other people we "have a *default to truth*: our operating assumption is that the people we are dealing with are honest" (2019, 73, Gladwell's emphasis). That is the expectation toward others involved in the definition of basic trust given above, and it is included in positive prejudice, though the latter involves more.

In his primer on trust, Borum defines trust "*as a willingness to accept vulnerability and risk based on confident expectations regarding another person's behavior*," and this is important "*particularly in the context of limited information or high consequences for a betrayal of trust*" (2010, 1, original in italics). I defined prejudice above as the tendency to fill in the gap in our knowledge of the Other, thus the "limited information" in Borum's definition of trust is of interest here. When people try to fill in the gap with their stereotypical ideas or engage in microaggressions—as discussed in several contexts earlier, the person at the receiving end will find it difficult to trust. We develop "confident expectations" in the context of positive experiences, when we have been able to lead our lives with support or at least non-interference rather than hindrance from others.

Pertaining to the "high consequences," trust becomes all the more pivotal when we need the services of someone we don't know well. This is an example of role-oriented or "category-based trust" (Kramer 1999). As discussed above, we need to accept the distance in the relationship, yet we have to trust that the person will succeed in her role performance. In this case, our trust is "based on having sufficient knowledge" (Borum 2010, 14) of how the Other is going to behave. That is why professionals have licenses that assure us of their appropriate education and experience. Our doctor's license, experience and reputation lead us to trust her, and the air captain and bus driver each have their credentials that lead us to trust them. Furthermore, codes of ethics spell out professional standards whose violations lead to disciplinary action. Positive prejudice expects such credentials and thus prevents blind trust.

As discussed in chapter 4 on respect, we need to hold the other accountable. Penalty for wrongdoing is acknowledging accountability and thus is respectful toward someone who has done something wrong. But trust involves mutual accountability, as Giselsson again explains:

> Moral equality is assumed when human beings insist on accountability, for when they do so they are insisting that they are an end in themselves and that they are not means to another's ends. It is this insistence that they are an end, a limit to the other's will—just as the other is an end, a limit to their will—that is the recognition of a common equality and indeed of a common humanity. (Giselsson 2012, 200)

As positive prejudice accepts the Other with his different opinion and yet holds him accountable to ethical standards, it also allows one to bow out of a transaction when one is not sure of the Other's credentials, motivations, or skills for the services he offers. For example, once a doctor that I had been referred to asked me if I liked him. That odd question, and the fact that he wanted to sell me some product and hook me for a long term, led me both cognitively and emotionally to not trust him and consequently to the decision to not come back.

The other person has no more right to embezzle you than you have the right to embezzle him. The correlative tension between self and Other that Ricoeur emphasizes (Wallace 2002, 86) holds both accountable. Positive prejudice assumes that the Other is an ethical person unless proven otherwise, but when you don't know—when the gap in your knowledge of the Other is too wide—bowing out is respectful. There is nothing wrong in letting the stranger relationship prevail; one can part company, not agreeing and not trusting the person for a particular role performance, and still be respectful. We sometimes forget this in misplaced chumminess.[3]

The fact is that in the modern Western world we don't know most of the people we do business with, so most of the time we deal with strangers. That brings to the fore the question of trust backed up with little knowledge. While knowing a stranger's credentials helps us trust her enough for a particular role performance in spite of the risk, positive prejudice respects the Other even if we find her credentials inadequate and thus refuse her services. Positive prejudice, then, includes more than the basic trust in the Other's innocent intentions; it includes accountability. We don't need to let the Other impinge on our freedom to act according to our priorities—as long as it doesn't hurt others. True, the car salesman may make one less sale if we don't buy in spite of his friendly gestures, and that will affect his family income, but I have to worry about my budget too and my family's needs. As Ricoeur holds, self and Other are in correlative tension in all our interactions. Respect and positive prejudice require paying attention to both parties.

That leads us to the type of trust in which the emotional component is prevalent. In their book on the social construction of trust, Weber and Carter define trust as "*an orientation* between self and other whose object is the relationship" (2003, 3, emphasis theirs). In their focus on close relationships, these authors feel that relationships with strangers do not involve trust per se. As discussed above, however, trust can be at different levels; prevalence of the cognitive dimension indicates trust in one's basic safety or the professional qualifications of those rendering services, whereas in closer relationships trust is based on more diffuse qualities of the other person. In this case we may know the Other as a kind and capable individual whose intentions and judgment are always good, and with whom we may have a bond.

But the emotional or affective component can also lead one into blind trust. Sometimes there is a "desire to be part of a collective or group" (Borum 2010, 15) that may lead a person to join a cult, for example. Or one may be swayed by someone's particularly charming qualities and forget the mutuality requirement in real trust. It is obvious from Gladwell's analysis of Chamberlain's trust of Hitler that the latter's charisma led the British prime minister astray; other politicians who had not met Hitler at all did not trust him. The above-mentioned sales people's efforts at personalizing commercial encounters also rely on this emotional component of trust, often creating anything else but trust. Positive prejudice would still accept the salesman as a valuable individual, but recognizing the gap in our knowledge of him would prevent blind trust.

Some people are by nature more trusting than others, and though this characteristic may make them pleasant companions, it may make them more gullible. A respondent in Weber and Carter's research described her "weak point" as "I'm going to trust you until you do something to me not to trust you." And she continued, "it's what works for me. . . . I trust everyone. I always think that everyone is good." Overall, she described herself as "a very caring, loving kind of person" (2003, 27). That woman definitely showed positive prejudice, but does that mean we should blindly trust everyone in every situation? The caution I mentioned above would indicate not. There are situations in which reason must override emotion.

The behavioral component refers to how we demonstrate trust in our actions. This may be the result of a rational decision—based on the cognitive component, though it could be an example of pure sociability—the affective component—as well (Borum 2010, 25). To use another one of Gladwell's examples, president Spanier, head coach Paterno, and other officials at Pennsylvania State University could not believe that their beloved colleague, coach Jerry Sandusky, was abusing boys. Sandusky was an admired and respected member of the university community. The emotional component of their trust in their colleague led to their behavioral reluctance to take the accusations seriously. With enormous amounts of data available, "the brain tends to pick up what it deems most salient . . . in order to make the best decision under the circumstances" (Borum 2010, 26). The situational circumstances—such as Sandusky's well-known and apparently innocent interest in and love of children—led these officials for nearly a decade to give him the benefit of the doubt in spite of objective information, as parents and counselors had done in earlier years.[4] They thought they knew Sandusky very well, but there was a serious gap in their knowledge of him that led to problems in their behavioral response to the situation.

Trust includes risk and vulnerability, as some incidents have shown, but most of the time our trust has been honored. As the example of trusting fellow travelers illustrates, we often "tend to take trust for granted" and "underrate" its significance because of our "strong tendency not to notice it until it breaks down" (Govier 1998, 5). Unfortunately, however, African Americans—especially young males—cannot take trust for granted because it has broken down too many times. Coates describes how "the culture of the streets" always made him cautious because that culture was "concerned chiefly with securing the body" (2015, 24). And as mentioned earlier regarding Coates's experiences and feelings, officers who were supposed to provide security became a perceived danger.

There are unfortunately plenty of other examples of trust breaking down. One only needs to follow the daily news for one story after another, and Gladwell's above-mentioned book analyzes a number of them. Neville Chamberlain's trust in Hitler helped bring about World War Two and the Holocaust; Ana Belen Montes, though trusted by the CIA, turned out to be a spy for Cuba; and many people who had invested with Bernard Madoff ended up losing their life savings. At a more subtle level, interactions—such as microaggressions—can erode trust and lead one to withhold from social life with strangers. Nadal cites research in which people experiencing micro-aggressions report "depressive symptoms and a negative view of the world" (2014, 73). A person's trust needs to be honored for it to survive, and in the final analysis, as Gladwell also acknowledges, "the alternative—to abandon trust as a defense against predation and deception—is worse" (2019, 343).

I suggested earlier that when one doesn't trust one could walk away from the situation. This may work in accepting or not accepting someone's professional services, but in many situations walking away is not an option. Perhaps you are in a committed relationship in which trust has been broken, and walking away is not that simple. Or you are forced to work every day with a person you cannot trust. That can lead to a complex situation that is not easy to handle. The difficult person needs to be respected, but you need to respect yourself too. Perhaps in that case a wise manager will try to rearrange the working situation; maybe a competent but uncooperative worker can be given a solo assignment. Yet avoidance, whenever possible, may be the best option in situations where trust has broken down.

At any rate, life is not ideal; compromises are often called for. Trust has its limits, but even then positive prejudice includes the expectation of mutual accountability, even if it means the end of a relationship, penalty for wrong-doing, or avoidance of certain geographical districts. While trust makes social life possible, its absence or shakiness reminds us that human life with other humans is not perfect. The more positive prejudice is practiced, however, the better will life be for everyone. It will also lead to structural changes that will make trust and safety possible for all people.

ETHICAL ENCOUNTERS

Chapter 1 briefly introduced a few major schools of thought in social ethics, all of which point to our moral obligation to gear our conduct in a way that can empower others to reach their best potential. Teleological ethics looks at that as a goal to achieve, while deontological ethics focuses on the rules for such ethical conduct, and virtue ethics sees the moral character of the acting person as pivotal. According to classical philosophy, such character encompasses wisdom, justice, courage, and temperance, and all of this includes the teleological aim of helping not only oneself but also the other person to flourish (Christian Smith 2010, 385, 406). Thus, according to all ethical theories, a good person does the right thing in a way that helps others realize their potential. Smith discusses the centrality of virtues as one of the key elements of moral life: "Moral virtues are those dispositions and practices that foster the achievement of the telos of persons. Moral vices and evils—either exercised by persons themselves or by others around them—are those that deflect or frustrate persons from realizing their purpose, which compromise, damage, negate, endanger, deny, or tear down the true nature of people's personhood" (2010, 402).

Smith further asserts that achieving full personhood of oneself and others is the aim, telos, and this can be realized only in community (2010, 406–8). MacIntyre makes a similar point. According to him, the Enlightenment project had to fail because it lacked telos, which is for humans to reach their potentiality and to realize it in action (MacIntyre 1984, 52). Care ethics, on the other hand, focuses explicitly on the relational nature of human life, our connectedness and interdependence that calls for our conduct to empower others to achieve their basic level of social functioning (Nussbaum 2000; Engster 2007). As mentioned in chapter 1, I see such basic level of functioning to include faith in oneself, and that is acquired largely by others' faith in us. Overall, communal ethics is about advancing the good for other people, which simultaneously includes reaching toward one's own potentiality. Our everyday interactions have a potential to enhance this.

Religious people generally consider themselves to be morally good persons who exemplify the virtue ethics. Yet, as my research on religious charity shows, not every kind of helping meets the criteria discussed in this book in terms of respect for the recipients of help. A Reformed Jewish rabbi explained his ethic in the following way: "Christianity operates out of a love ethic; Judaism operates out of an obligation ethic. I don't give because I love the next person; I give because I have to" (Terian 1984, 274). The same rabbi criticized a woman in a grocery line paying with food stamps for frozen noodles, which he considered a too expensive way to get nutritional benefits. A Catholic young woman in charge of her church's welfare work, on the other hand, refused to criticize the needy families that had color televisions, acknowledging that in their lack of entertainment and transportation, they need a color television more than the wealthy do (1984, 286). It needs to be noted that in this research the differences were less on denominational lines than in individual approaches. There is plenty of loving concern in Jewish ethics, and there are Catholic moralizers as well. But as psychologists have observed, doing charitable work with the feeling of obligation or do-goodism is "benefiting another as a means to benefit oneself"—a special form of egoism (Batson 2010, 17). Also, such approach often inadvertently blames the victims for their condition. True love ethic and justice ethic leave ego aside, and they go hand in hand in respecting the recipient of help.

Some people are so eager to help that they often go to what the social psychologist Dolly Chugh calls a "savior mode" when they meet other people. "Saviors like problems because we get to solve them," she observes, "but when we are in savior mode, we forget that there are real people behind the problems. When I am in savior mode, I otherize the very people I want to support, prioritizing my needs over theirs." The sympathy mode may sound better, but it "is much like the savior mode, . . . less about solving the problem and more about being the one who does not have the problem" (Chugh 2018, 152). Moreover, "sympathy can also backfire for the target of our sympathy. If the person believes our actions are born of sympathy and not of their merit, their self-esteem and motivation takes [*sic*] a hit" (Chugh 2018, 154). That has been my concern throughout this book. According to Chugh, empathy is better: "Empathy works the other way. We allow ourselves to feel what is happening in the circle. We allow the feeling to spill out of the circle or we are willing to enter the circle. Our attention is centered on what others are feeling, not on what we are feeling. Empathy leads to behaviors allies strive for" (2018, 153).

Even in the best of circumstances and with the best of the "do-gooder's" intentions, psychologists have noted that receiving help is "a mixed blessing"; while being "a message of caring" it is also "self-threatening" (Nadler et al. 2010, 183). An emergency situation may be an exception because the recipient's status is not threatened. Another exception is a situation where the disadvantaged position "is perceived as both legitimate and stable," then "being helped is not self-threatening." But under perceivable unstable or illegitimate status differences, "recipients desire and expect equality, and being helped is inconsistent with these expectations and therefore self-threatening" (Nadler et al. 2010, 195). At the bottom of these dynamics is the fact that helping relations are power relations (Nadler et al. 2010, 197).

The point is that ethical behavior toward other people—whether they need our help or not—is to focus on the Other. That does not mean being in the "savior mode" and looking for problems to solve, but it does mean doing our best to look at the situation from the Other's viewpoint. The organizational psychologist Adam Grant (2013) has shown that a giving spirit that allows others to succeed—even at one's own expense—often leads to one's own success in the long run, and it creates a "ripple effect" (2013, 10) that inspires others and improves the climate of the organization as a whole. This is a prime example of positive prejudice empowering others.

Race and ethnic relations is another area where "morally good" people often display a lack of understanding. As discussed in chapter 4, the Enlightenment philosophy with its universalism erred in not respecting difference.

Thus many well-meaning people, including myself, have made mistakes in viewing color-blindness as the ethical goal. On the surface, it seems fair and just to call for equal treatment of everyone with no regard for differences. Organizations advertize that as a goal in hiring. But that inadvertently hides the identities and experiences of people who are different, so the "equal treatment" is no longer equal. Accepting our own "situated understanding" (Sandel 2014, 70) requires also seeing the Other in context to get a more accurate picture. Chugh quotes an African American college student: "If you don't see my color, you deny who I am. You deny so much that is wonderful about me. You deny the struggles I've been through. You deny me" (2018, 156). Black or brown is beautiful, and positive prejudice sees the beauty in the difference and takes the Other's circumstances into account.

The same principle applies to equal treatment of women. Even though things have improved, unequal treatment based on gender is still prevalent. Sometimes women in sports have complained that they were paid only half-a-million, for example, when men got three quarters of a million. Some people have remarked that these women had no reason to complain because half-a-million a year is a lot of money. But the point is that they were made to feel inferior, and that was not respectful. Another example comes from higher education in nineteenth-century United States: Oberlin College, the first to admit women, required women to do male students' laundry, clean their rooms and serve their meals, in addition to caring for themselves and doing their studies (Flexner 1971). At hearing this, one man remarked: "Aren't you glad that you don't have to do that?" In other words, "You have come a long way, baby! You should be happy." That is equivalent to saying to an African American, "Aren't you glad that you're not a slave any more?" As every member of a marginalized group knows, such "congratulations" not only miss the point but also offend because they do not assume equal human worth. The demand for respect to which every human is entitled cannot be satisfied with anything less than equal respect for people in different categories, be they different genders, ethnic groups, or social classes.

Responding to negative prejudice and the microaggressions described above is an ethical dilemma that presents an additional burden to the person at the receiving end. To maintain one's self-esteem and mutual respect (see chapter 4), some response is necessary, yet not all types of responses are helpful. In a multicultural research, Michéle Lamont with coauthors interviewed people about their responses. In the United States, most African Americans would confront the person who has behaved in a stigmatizing or discriminating way, while others would not respond. One respondent said, "I'm bo-jangling and tap dancing." Thirty percent mentioned management of self-preservation, with one person "doing a lot more smiling" and trying to conform to expectations. Almost a third mentioned the importance of managing their anger and "picking their battles." Other responses involved religion, hard work, education, and self-improvement (Lamont et al. 2016, 92–94).

Even worse is a situation in which one person is railroading things on another, backing the Other into a corner that doesn't leave a way out. What is the best way to preserve dignity in such a case? To always acquiesce is detrimental to self-esteem, so is throwing a tantrum. Mutual respect is challenging in this case. Calm refusal seems the only good response, accompanied by an explanation that does not accuse the other as a person but uses I-statements. The point is that experiencing negative prejudice, discrimination, and unequal power relationships makes interpersonal encounters unnecessarily heavy and challenging to self-respect. This is the more demanding side of ethical encounters.

No one is perfect, however, in the interpersonal realm any more than in other realms. Chugh uses the term "bounded ethicality" to describe normal people who are basically good and have the "moral identity" of a good person but sometimes lapse as all of us do. So morality is not a binary notion; all of us are "good-ish people" (2018, 7–8). We need to engage in "ethical learning" and each day try to do better, have a "growing mindset" (Chugh 2018, 23). Achieving the good in ourselves and in society is a "quest," a continuous movement that does not allow stagnation; one either progresses or regresses (Christian Smith 2010, 401–2). Or as Gadamer reflects, "our horizons are at every moment evolving. . . . The infinity reflects the projective character of understanding, its endless potential to develop itself" (1982, 183). With humility we all need to acknowledge our imperfections and strive to do better, and to become more generous in forgiving others' shortcomings. Many books on prejudice and trust, interestingly, include chapters on forgiveness (e.g., Tropp and Mallett 2011; Govier 1998; Weber and Carter 2003). In our imperfect world, positive prejudice requires humility and forgiveness.

CONCLUSION

The purpose of this book has been to put the concept of prejudice in a larger context, show its place in human perception and understanding, and point a way to its positive form. The first chapter explained how the construction and maintenance of self is a social endeavor, and how self-esteem is dependent on constructive feedback from others. Without receiving recognition of one's value as a person and other positive feedback, one easily entertains self-doubt and thus is not able to be one's best self. In our interactions, we need to acknowledge the Other as a subject, a separate self, an agency with her own goals and priorities. Objectification makes many ostensibly innocent interactions threats to the Other's self, whereas ethical interactions support one's own self and work toward enhancing the autonomy and agency of other selves.

The practical dimensions of these concepts were brought forth in the second chapter that looked at interpersonal encounters. We take our daily encounters with other people for granted, but in reality these encounters are complicated events that have the potential of enhancing or frustrating not only other people's days but also their motivations and faith in themselves. As members of the same human species, our existential situation and shared symbols give us a common horizon, yet the different cultural, structural, historical, and personal background factors of each participant present challenges to the encounter. Recognizing the otherness of the Other and his different life circumstances gives us humility and helps us tread softly with other people. The ethical challenge is to remember the difference and not assume that we know the Other, even in close relationships.

The first two chapters provided the background to the main subject of the book, prejudice, which was taken up in the third chapter. Prejudicial attitudes expressed by others make a difference in the development and maintenance of one's self, and prejudice definitely appears in interpersonal encounters, from perception to behavior. Contrary to calls for eliminating prejudice, however, a comprehensive look at the meaning and historical development of the concept shows its place in all perception. Therefore it could not be eliminated but could be shaped into a positive form. By first acknowledging one's negative attitude toward the Other and realizing one's lack of objective knowledge about the Other, by correcting one's initial perceptions, enlarging one's ingroup, and calling forth one's higher values, one can change prejudice from negative to positive. Obviously, this is not something that can be done instantaneously; it is a quest, an aim to strive for, a telos, and ethical life requires us to take up that quest. The reward is richer and more meaningful life for everyone involved.

Respect is an integral part of positive prejudice, as chapter 4 was intended to show. Such respect is based on the status of the Other as a human being, apart from her qualities or achievements, though these too need to be recognized in family, community, and society. Respect means seeing each person as an end in herself, and not as mere means for someone else's end. It also means that each person is a free agent who is accountable for her actions— each is accountable to the Other and to the community, and respect requires acknowledging that accountability. Though the Enlightenment idea of universal rights is the foundation of the ethical principle of respect for persons, it did not include respect for difference. Thus true respect needs to go beyond universalism to the appreciation of each person's and group's special identity, history, struggles, and unique qualities. In other words, respect requires not only recognition of universal human rights but also attention to the particular needs and qualities of minority individuals and groups. Thus both universalism and particularism are needed for respect, and this takes place in a community of mutual respect and accountability. Respect or the lack of it shows in our everyday interactions and therefore presents an ethical challenge to all our relationships.

In this last chapter, I have tried to provide a closure to the discussion by examining the major concepts, prejudice and respect, from other angles and with a somewhat critical eye. Defining prejudice as an attempt to fill in the gap in our knowledge of the Other, this chapter emphasized the need to accept the gap—if getting acquainted is not an option—and respect the Other in the status of a stranger. That is positive prejudice, and it also accepts the fact that even in close relationships we really don't know the Other. Thus caution is in order in all our relationships, but more so when the gap is wide. The idea of positive prejudice could easily be seen as blind trust in the Other, but this need not be so if the relationship is not defined in too close terms. In the commercial world, there is often an attempt to show emotional closeness in order to make a sale, but respecting the Other need not mean blind trust in a person we know little about. Maintaining distance in the encounter can still include a positive attitude that is respectful.

The idea of "situated understanding" (Sandel 2014) shows the role of prejudice in all our perceptions. Recognizing this factor helps us halt the process of defining the Other, refrain from further filling in the gap, and correct the initial misconception. The road toward positive prejudice parts from the negative type at this juncture. It means to cast doubt on our "stock of knowledge" regarding the type of person we are meeting and willingness to see the world from his viewpoint, seeing him as an equally viable member of our shared community. While prejudice allowed us to perceive and helped us in our initial understanding, we must acknowledge the possibility that we may be wrong in our perception and assessment. A humble acceptance of the limitations of our knowledge and perception meets the other person at a level playing field, and that is respectful.

In this book, I have examined the concept of prejudice at the intersection of three different areas of inquiry: social psychology, phenomenology, and social ethics. Overall, writing this book has been my attempt to understand the role of prejudice in our daily life and in all our interactions. Particularly, I have sought to explain its great effect on our self-respect, vitality, and ability to work toward our goals. Traditionally, prejudice has been defined as a social problem that—regardless of many ideas and efforts for its reduction or elimination—has eluded solution, as countless examples show. Looking at the concept in its larger meaning provides the idea of its positive form. With this broader view, the goal is not the elimination of prejudice but greater understanding of its nature that will help us gear our attitudes toward others in a positive direction. As is increasingly acknowledged in psychological literature as well, such positive attitude is much more promising than the old calls for eliminating prejudice that often emphasized tolerance as a goal. Positive prejudice goes far beyond tolerance, and respect for persons means respect for difference, something that is increasingly needed in today's multicultural world. Ethical encounters help empower the partners, and positive prejudice has the potential for increasing such encounters in everyday life.

NOTES

1. Levinas makes that point in several contexts. For example, describing the "exteriority of the face," he (1987, 107) states that the face of the other calls forth "the rupture of phenomenology."

2. Borum (2010, 46, 51–52) cites extensive crosscultural research that shows variation in generalized interpersonal trust in different countries. In one study, Sweden, China, and the United States were high on the propensity to trust, whereas Russia, India, and Mexico were moderate and Romania and Brazil were low (Johnson and Cullen 2002).

3. We do, however, exercise caution by instructing children not to trust or even talk to strangers.

4. Decades earlier, Sandusky had founded a charity called the Second Mile, a recreational program for troubled boys that had helped thousands of boys from poor and often single-parent homes. One boy's mother even referred to Sandusky as "some sort of angel" (Gladwell 2019, 114, 116).

References

Abraham, Melissa. 2019. "UCLA receives $20 million to establish UCLA Bedari Kindness Institute." UCLA Newsroom, press release. September 25, 2019.

Allport, Gordon W. (1954) 1958. *The Nature of Prejudice: A Comprehensive and Penetrating Study of the Origin and Nature of Prejudice.* Garden City, NY: Doubleday, Anchor Books. Original by Addison-Wesley Publishing Co.

Althusser, Louis. 2001. "Ideology and Ideological State Apparatuses." Translated by Ben Brewster. In *Lenin and Philosophy and Other Essays*, 127–88. New York: Monthly Review Press.

Antich, Peter. 2018. "Merleau-Ponty's Theory of Preconceptual Generalities and Concept Formation." *History of Philosophy Quarterly* 35 (3): 279–97.

Apel, Otto A. 1997. "Plurality of the Good? The Problem of Affirmative Tolerance in a Multicultural Society from an Ethical Point of View." *Ratio Juris* 10: 199–222.

Aviram, Ron B. 2009. *The Relational Origins of Prejudice: A Convergence of Psychoanalytic and Social Cognitive Perspectives.* Lanham, MD: Jason Aronson, a subsidiary of Rowman & Littlefield.

Badger, Philip. 2010. "What's Wrong with the Enlightenment?" *Philosophy Now 2019.*http://philosophynow.org/search?q=prejudice

Batson, C. Daniel. 2010. "Empathy-Induced Altruistic Motivation." In *Prosocial Motives, Emotions, and Behavior*, edited by Marion Mikulincer and Phillip R. Shaver, 15–34. Washington, DC: American Psychological Association.

Baumeister, Roy F., ed. 1999. *The Self in Social Psychology.* Philadelphia, PA: Psychology Press (Taylor & Francis).

Belmont Report. 1979. https://www.hhs.gov/ohrp/regulations-and-policy/belmont-report/read-the-belmont-report/index.html

Benson, Kyle. 2017. "The Magic Relationship Ratio, According to Science." The Gottman Relationship Bloc, www.Gottman.com (accessed October 4, 2017).

Ben-Zeev, Aaron. 2009. "Darling, Does Your Tolerance of Me Imply That You Do Not Love Me? Can Love Involve Tolerance?" https://www.psychologytoday.com/us/blog/in-the-name-of-love-does-your tolerance-toward-me-imply-you-do-not-love-me

Berger, Peter L. and Thomas Luckmann. (1966) 1967. *The Social Construction of Reality: A Treatise in the Sociology of Knowledge.* New York: Doubleday Anchor Books.

Bonilla-Silva, Eduardo. 2017. *Racism without Racists: Color-Blind Racism and the Persistence of Racial Inequality in America.* Fifth edition. Lanham, MD: Rowman & Littlefield.

Borum, Randy. 2010. "The Science of Interpersonal Trust." *Mental Health Law and Policy Faculty Publications.* 574. http://scholarcommons.usf.edu/mhlp_facpub/574

Brown, Brené. 2015. *Rising Strong: The Reckoning, the Rumble, the Revolution.* New York: Spiegel & Grau.

Brown, Rupert. 2010. *Prejudice: Its Social Psychology.* Second edition. West Sussex, UK: Wiley-Blackwell.

Buber, Martin. 1970. *I and Thou.* New York: Scribner.

Burrow, Rufus Jr. 1999. *Personalism: A Critical Introduction.* St. Louis, MO: Chalice Press.

Butz, David A. and E. Ashby Plant. 2011. "Approaching versus Avoiding Intergroup Contact: The Role of Expectancies and Motivation." In *Moving Beyond Prejudice Reduction: Pathways to Positive Intergroup Relations*, edited by Linda R. Tropp and Robyn K. Mallett, 81–98. Washington, DC: American Psychological Association.

Campbell, Bradley and Jason Manning. 2018. *The Rise of Victimhood Culture: Microaggressions, Safe Spaces, and the New Culture Wars.* Cham, Switzerland: Palgrave Macmillan.

Carman, Taylor. 2012. "Foreword." In *Phenomenology of Perception* by Maurice Merleau-Ponty, vii–xvi. New York: Routledge.

Chen, Jacqueline M. and Kate A. Ratliff. 2018. "Psychological Essentialism Predicts Intergroup Bias." *Social Cognition* 36 (3): 301–23.

Cheryan, Sapna and Galen V. Bodenhausen. 2000. "When Positive Stereotypes Threaten Intellectual Performance: The Psychological Hazards of "Model Minority" Status." *Psychological Science* 11: 399–402.

Christakis, Nicholas A. 2019. *Blueprint: The Evolutionary Origins of a Good Society.* New York: Little, Brown Spark.

Chugh, Dolly. 2018. *The Person You Mean to Be: How Good People Fight Bias.* New York: HarperCollins.

Coates, Ta-Nehisi. 2015. *Between the World and Me.* New York: Spiegel & Grau.

Cohen, Richard. 1987. "Introduction" to Emanuel Levinas, *Time and the Other.* Translated by Richard A. Cohen. Pittsburgh, PA: Duquesne University Press.

———. 2003. "Introduction" to Emanuel Levinas, *Humanism of the Other.* Urbana and Chicago: University of Illinois Press.

Cole, Nicki Lisa. 2020. "How Sociologists Define Human Agency." ThoughtCo, January 29, 2020. thoughtco.com/agency-definition-3026036

Cooley, Charles Horton. 1902. *Human Nature and the Social Order.* New York: Charles Scribner's Sons.

Cusk, Rachel. 2017. "The Age of Rudeness: As the Social Contract Frays, What Does It Mean to Be Polite?" *The New York Times Magazine*, February 15, 2017. https://www.nytimes.com/2017/02/15/magazine/the-age-of-rudeness.html

Darwall, Stephen. 2006. *The Second Person Standpoint: Morality, Respect and Accountability.* Cambridge, MA and London: Harvard University Press.

Davies, Kristin, Stephen C. Wright, and Arthur Aron. 2011. "Cross-Group Friendships: How Interpersonal Connections Encourage Positive Intergroup Attitudes." In *Moving Beyond Prejudice Reduction: Pathways to Positive Intergroup Relations*, edited by Linda R. Tropp and Robyn K. Mallett, 119–38. Washington, DC: American Psychological Association.

deBotton, Alain. 2016. "Why You Will Marry the Wrong Person." *The New York Times*, Sunday Review Opinion, May 28, 2016.

Derrida, Jacques. 1973. *Speech and Phenomena: And Other Essays on Husserl's Theory of Signs.* Evanston, IL: Northwestern University Press.

Dorschel, Andreas. 2000. *Rethinking Prejudice.* Burlington, VT: Ashgate.

Dovidio, John F., Miles Hewstone, Peter Glick, and Victoria M. Esses. 2010. "Prejudice, Stereotyping and Discrimination: Theoretical and Empirical Overview." In *The Sage Handbook of Prejudice, Stereotyping and Discrimination*, edited by John F. Dovidio, Miles Hewstone, Peter Glick, and Victoria M. Esses, 3–28. London: Sage.

Dovidio, John F., Kerry Kawakami, Craig Johnson, Brenda Johnson, and Adaiah Howard. 1997. "On the Nature of Prejudice: Automatic and Controlled Processes." *Journal of Experimental Social Psychology* 33 (5): 510–40.

Duckworth, Angela. 2016. *Grit: The Power of Passion and Perseverance.* New York: Scribner.

Durkheim, Emile. 1912. *The Elementary Forms of the Religious Life.* New York: Macmillan.

Dworkin, Andrea. 1974. *Woman Hating: A Radical Look at Sexuality.* Boston: E. P. Dutton.

Ebren, Figen. 2009. "Susceptibility to Interpersonal Influence: A Study in Turkey." *Social Behavior and Personality: An International Journal* 37 (8): 1051–63.

Eisenberg, Nancy. 2010. "Empathy-Related Responding: Links with Self-Regulation, Moral Judgment, and Moral Behavior." In *Prosocial Motives, Emotions, and Behavior*, edited by Marion Mikulincer and Phillip R. Shaver, 129–48. Washington, DC: American Psychological Association.

Emirbayer, Mustafa, and Ann Mische. 1998. "What Is Agency?" *American Journal of Sociology* 103 (4): 962–1023.

Engster, Daniel. 2007. *The Heart of Justice: Care Ethics and Political Theory*. New York: Oxford University Press.

Erikson, Erik H. 1963. *Childhood and Society*. Second edition. New York: W. W. Norton.

Fanon, Franz. 1967. *Black Skin, White Masks*. New York: Grove Press.

Fehr, Beverley. 2010. "Compassionate Love as a Prosocial Emotion." In *Prosocial Motives, Emotions, and Behavior*, edited by Marion Mikulincer and Phillip R. Shaver, 245–65. Washington, DC: American Psychological Association.

Firestone, Robert W. and Joyce Catlett. 2009. *The Ethics of Interpersonal Relationships*. London: Karnac Books, Ltd.

Fiske, Susan T. 1992. "Stereotypes Work . . . But Only Sometimes: Comment on How to Motivate the 'Unfinished Mind.'" *Psychological Inquiry* 3: 161–62.

Flexner, Eleanor. 1959. *Century of Struggle: The Women's Rights Movement in the United States*. Cambridge, MA: Belknap Press of Harvard University Press.

Foucault, Paul-Michel. 1971. *The Order of Things: An Archaeology of the Human Sciences*. New York: Pantheon Books. French original: *les mots et les choses: Une archeology des sciences humaines*, 1966.

Fraser, Nancy and Axel Honneth. 2003. *Redistribution or Recognition? A Political-Philosophical Exchange*. Translated by Joel Golb, James Ingram, and Christiane Wilke. London: Verso.

Freire, Paulo. (1970) 1992. *Pedagogy of the Oppressed*. New York: Continuum.

Freud, Sigmund. 1923. *Das Ich und das Es (The Ego and the Id)*. Leipzig: Internationaler Psychoanalytischer Verlag. Reprinted in his *Gesammelte Werke* (London: Imago, 1940) 13: 237–89.

Friedersdorf, Conor. 2015. "The Rise of Victimhood Culture." *Atlantic: Web Edition Articles (USA)*, September 11, 2015. *Newsbank: America's News—Historical and Current*. https://www.infoweb-newsbank-com.proxy.lib.duke.edu/apps/news/document-view?p=AMNEWS&docref=news/157D419216979990

Gadamer, Hans-Georg. (1975) 1982. *Truth and Method*. New York: Crossroad. 1975 publication by Sheed and Ward Ltd.

Gaertner, Samuel L., John F. Dovidio, and Melissa A. Houlette. 2010. "Social Categorization." In *The Sage Handbook of Prejudice, Stereotyping and Discrimination*, edited by John F. Dovidio, Miles Hewstone, Peter Glick, and Victoria M. Esses, 526–43. London: Sage.

Galeotti, Anna Elisabetta. 2002. *Toleration as Recognition*. Cambridge: Cambridge University Press.

Gibson, James J. 1979. *The Ecological Approach to Visual Perception*. Boston: Houghton Mifflin.

Gilligan, Carol. 1982. *In a Different Voice: Psychological Theory and Women's Development*. Cambridge, MA: Harvard University Press.

Giselsson, Kristi. 2012. *Grounds for Respect: Particularism, Universalism, and Communal Accountability*. Lanham, MD: Lexington Books, subsidiary of Rowman & Littlefield.

Gladwell, Malcolm. 2019. *Talking to Strangers: What We Should Know about the People We Don't Know*. New York: Little, Brown and Company.

Glanville, Doug. 2014. "I Was Racially Profiled in My Own Driveway." *Atlantic Web Edition Articles (USA)*, April 14, 2014. *Newsbank: America's News—Historical and Current*. https://infoweb-newsbank-com.proxy.lib.duke.edu/apps/news/document-view?p=AMNEWS&docref=news/I4D38263B62D6668

Goffman, Erving. 1959. *The Presentation of Self in Everyday Life*. New York: Doubleday.

————. 1961. *Encounters: Two Studies in the Sociology of Interaction.* Indianapolis, IN: Bobb-Merrill.

————. 1967. *Interaction Ritual.* Garden City, NY: Anchor Books.

————. 1983. "The Interaction Order." *American Sociological Review* 48: 1–17.

Goodnough, Abby. 2009. "Harvard Professor Jailed; Officer Accused of Bias." *The New York Times* online. https://www.nytimes.com/2009/07/21/us/21gates.html

Gottman, John M. 1994. *Why Marriages Succeed or Fail.* New York: Simon & Schuster.

Govier, Trudy. 1998. *Dilemmas of Trust.* Montreal: McGill-Queen's University Press.

Grant, Adam. 2013. *Give and Take: The Hidden Social Dynamics of Success.* New York: Viking.

Green, Leslie. 2010. "Two Worries about Respect for Persons." *Ethics* 120, no. 2 (January): 212–31.

Habermas, Jürgen. 1987. *A Theory of Communicative Action.* Vol. II in *Lifeworld and System: A Critique of Functionalist Reason.* Translated by Thomas McCarthy. Boston: Beacon Press.

Hahn, Adam, Charles M. Judd, Holen K. Hirsh, and Irene V. Blair. 2014. "Awareness of Implicit Attitudes." *Journal of Experimental Psychology: General* 143 (3): 1369–92. http://dx.doi.org/10.1037/a0035028

Haraway, Donna. 1988. "Situated Knowledges: The Science Question in Feminism and the Privilege of Partial Perspective." *Feminist Studies* 14 (3): 575–99.

Hardy, Thomas. (1874) 1993. *Far from the Madding Crowd.* Hertfordshire, UK: Wordsworth Editions Limited.

Harman, Danna. 2019. "Afghan Robotics Team Sees a Different World." *The New York Times*, International, Vol. CLXVIII (no. 58,282, March 30, 2019): A6–A7.

Harris, George W. 1997. *Dignity and Vulnerability: Strength and Quality of Character.* Berkeley: University of California Press.

Heidegger, Martin. 1962. *Being and Time.* Translated by John Macquarrie and Edward Robinson. New York: Harper and Row.

Hess, Amanda. 2016. "Is 'Empathy' Really What the Nation Needs?" *The New York Times* online (nytimes.com), November 29, 2016. https://www.nytimes.com/2016/11/29/magazine/is-empathy-really-what-the-nation-needs.html

Hill, Thomas E. 1973. "Servility and Self-Respect." *Monist* 57: 87–140.

Hilton, James L. and William von Hippel. 1996. "Stereotypes." *Annual Review of Psychology* 47: 237–71.

Honneth, Alex. 1996. *The Struggle for Recognition: The Moral Grammar of Social Conflicts.* Translated by Joel Anderson. Cambridge, MA: The MIT Press.

————. 2012. *The I in We: Studies in the Theory of Recognition.* Translated by Joseph Ganahl. Cambridge, UK: Polity Press.

Hopkins, Jack. 1983. "Judge's Order Depriving Parents of Son Is Upheld." *Seattle Post-Intelligencer*, 1. June 7, 1983.

Howe, David. 2013. *Empathy: What It Is and Why It Matters.* New York: Palgrave Macmillan.

Hugenberg, Kurt, and Galen V. Bodenhausen. 2003. "Facing Prejudice: Implicit Prejudice and the Perception of Facial Threat." *Psychological Science* 14 (6): 640–43 (accessed through JSTOR).

Iser, Mattias. 2013. "Recognition." *The Stanford Encyclopedia of Philosophy* (Fall edition), edited by Edward N. Zalta. https://plato.stanford.edu/entries/recognition/

Johnson, Jean L. and John B. Cullen. 2002. "Trust in Cross-Cultural Relationships." In *The Blackwell Handbook of Cross-Cultural Management*, edited by Martin J. Gannon and Karen Newman, 335–60. Oxford: Blackwell.

Jones, Melinda. 2002. *Social Psychology of Prejudice.* Upper Saddle River, NJ: Prentice Hall.

Kant, Immanuel. 1952. *The Critique of Judgment.* Translated by James Creed Meredith. Oxford: Oxford University Press. First published 1790.

————. 1964. *Groundwork of the Metaphysics of Morals.* Translated and analyzed by H(erbert) J. Paton. New York: Harper & Row, Harper Torchbooks.

————. 1991. *Political Writings* (Second, enlarged edition). Edited by Hans S. Reiss and translated by H. B(arry) Nisbet. Cambridge: Cambridge University Press.

Kay, Aaron C., Martin V. Day, Mark P. Zanna, and A. David Nussbaum. 2013. "The Insidious (and Ironic) Effects of Positive Stereotypes." *Journal of Experimental Social Psychology* 49: 287–91. https://doi.org/10.1016/j.jesp.2012.11.003

Keller, Mitch. 2006. "The Scandal at the Zoo," *The New York Times,* August 6, 2006. https://www.nytimes.com/2006/08/06/nyregion/thecity/06zoo.html

Kenny, David A. 1994. *Interpersonal Perception: A Social Relations Analysis.* New York: The Guilford Press.

Kierkegaard, Søren. 1995. *Works of Love: Some Christian Reflections in the Form of Discourses.* Translated by Howard and Edna Hong. Princeton, NJ: Princeton University Press.

Knobloch, Leanne K. and Bethany Schmelzer. 2008. "Using the Emotion-in-Relationships Model to Predict Features of Interpersonal Influence Attempts." *Communication Monographs* 75 (3): 219–47.

Konstan, David. 2008. "Aristotle on Love and Friendship." Σχολή: *Journal of the Centre for Ancient Philosophy and the Classical Tradition* (University of Novosibirsk) 2 (2): 207–12.

Kramer, Roderick M. 1999. "Trust and Distrust in Organizations: Emerging Perspectives, Enduring Questions." *Annual Review of Psychology* 50: 569–98.

Krebs, Angelika. 2010. "Dialogical Love." ethics-etc.com/wp-content/uploads/2010/02/krebs.pdf. Accessed 02/05/2020

Kuhn, Thomas. (1962) 1996. *The Structure of Scientific Revolutions.* Third edition. Chicago: University of Chicago Press.

Kundu, Anindya. 2017. *Achieving Agency: Regaining Collective Responsibilities for All Students to Succeed.* Lanham, MD: Rowman & Littlefield.

Lachs, John. 2014. *Meddling: On the Virtue of Leaving Others Alone.* Bloomington: Indiana University Press.

Lamont, Michéle, Graciella Moraes Silva, Jessica S. Welburn, Josjhua Guetzkow, Nissim Mizrachi, Hanna Herzog, and Elisa Reis. 2016. *Getting Respect: Responding to Stigma and Discrimination in the United States, Brazil, and Israel.* Princeton, NJ: Princeton University Press.

Landes, Donald A. 2012. "Translator's Introduction." In *Phenomenology of Perception* by Maurice Merleau-Ponty, xxx–li. New York: Routledge.

Lawrence-Lightfoot, Sara. 1999. *Respect: An Exploration.* Cambridge, MA: Perseus Books.

Leslie, Ian. 2014. *Curious: The Desire to Know and Why Your Future Depends on It.* New York: Basic Books.

Levinas, Emmanuel. 1987. *Time and the Other.* Translated by Richard A. Cohen. Pittsburgh, Pennsylvania: Duquesne University Press. Originally published as "Le temps et l'autre," in J. Wahl, *Le Choix, Le Monde, L'Existence,* Grenoble-Paris: Arthaud, 1947.

———. 1991. *Otherwise Than Being or Beyond Essence.* Translated by Alphonso Lingis. Boston: Kluwer.

———. 1998. *On Thinking-of the-Other entre nous.* Translated from the French by Michael B. Smith and Barbara Harshav. New York: Columbia University Press. Original *Éntre Nous: Essais sur le penser-á-l'autre* © Editions Grasset & Fasquelle 1991.

———. 2003. *Humanism of the Other.* Translated from the French by Nidra Poller. Urbana and Chicago: University of Illinois Press. Original *Humanisme de l'autre homme,* by Editions Fata Morgana, 1972.

Lewis, J. David and Andrew J. Weigert. 1985. "Trust as a Social Reality." *Social Forces* 63: 967–85.

Lieberman, Matthew D. 2013. *Social: Why Our Brains Are Wired to Connect.* New York: Crown Publishers.

Lippman, Walter. 1922. *Public Opinion.* New York: Harcourt, Brace.

Livingston, Robert W. 2011. "What Can Tolerance Teach Us about Prejudice? Profiles of the Nonprejudiced." In *Moving Beyond Prejudice Reduction: Pathways to Positive Intergroup Relations,* edited by Linda R. Tropp and Robyn K. Mallett, 21–40. Washington, DC: American Psychological Association.

Loewenstein, George. 1994. "The Psychology of Curiosity: A Review and Reinterpretation." *Psychological Bulletin* 116 (1): 75–98.

López, José and Garry Potter, eds. 2001. *After Postmodernism: An Introduction to Critical Realism.* New York: The Athlone Press, a Continuum imprint.

Lyotard, Jean-Francois. 1984. *The Postmodern Condition: A Report on Knowledge.* Original French: *La condition postmoderne: Rapport sur le savoir,* 1979. Translated by Geoffrey Bennington and Brian Massumi. Minneapolis: University of Minnesota Press.

MacIntyre, Alasdair. 1984. *After Virtue: A Study in Moral Theory.* Second edition. Notre Dame, IN: University of Notre Dame Press.

Maclagan, W(illiam) G(auld). 1960. "Respect for Persons as a Moral Principle–I." *Philosophy: The Journal of the Royal Institute of Philosophy* 35 (134): 193–217.

———. 1960. "Respect for Persons as a Moral Principle–II." *Philosophy: The Journal of the Royal Institute of Philosophy* 35 (135): 289–305.

Major, Brenda and Sarah S. M. Townsend. 2010. "Coping with Bias." In *The Sage Handbook of Prejudice, Stereotyping and Discrimination,* edited by John F. Dovidio, Miles Hewstone, Peter Glick, and Victoria M. Esses, 410–25. London: Sage.

Malson, Lucien. 1972. *Wolf Children and the Problem of Human Nature.* New York: Monthly Review Press.

Manning, Tony, Graham Pogson, and Zoë Morrison. 2008. "Interpersonal Influence in the Workplace—Part Two: Some Research Findings—Influencing Behavior, Personality and Context." *Industrial and Commercial Training* 40 (4): 188–96.

Marton, Ference. 1988. "Phenomenography: Exploring Different Conceptions of Reality." In *Qualitative Approaches to Evaluation in Education: The Silent Scientific Revolution,* edited by David M. Fetterman, 176–205. New York: Praeger.

Mauss, Marcel. 1967. *The Gift: Forms and Functions of Exchange in Archaic Societies.* Translated by Ian Cunnison. New York: W. W. Norton.

McClean, Charles. 1978. *The Wolf Children.* New York: Hill & Wang.

Mead, George Herbert. 1934. *Mind, Self, and Society: From the Standpoint of a Social Behaviorist.* Edited by Charles W. Morris. Chicago: University of Chicago Press.

———. 1964. *Selected Writings.* Edited by Andrew J. Reck. Indianapolis: Library of the Liberal Arts.

Merleau-Ponty, Maurice. (1948) 2004. *The World of Perception.* Translated by Oliver Davis. London and New York: Routledge.

———. 2012. *Phenomenology of Perception.* Translated by Donald A. Landes. New York: Routledge, Taylor & Francis Group. Originally published as *Phénoménologie de la perception,* © Éditions GALLIMARD, Paris, 1945.

Meyers, Diana. 1993. "Moral Reflection: Beyond Impartial Reason." *Hypatia* 8, no. 3 (Summer): 21–47.

Migacheva, Katya, Linda R. Tropp, and Jennifer Crocker. 2011. "Focusing Beyond the Self: Goal Orientations in Intergroup Relations." In *Moving Beyond Prejudice Reduction: Pathways to Positive Intergroup Relations,* edited by Linda R. Tropp and Robyn K. Mallett, 99–115. Washington, DC: American Psychological Association.

Mikulincer, Marion and Phillip R. Shaver, eds. 2010. *Prosocial Motives, Emotions, and Behavior.* Washington, DC: American Psychological Association.

Miller, David. 1999. *Principles of Social Justice.* Cambridge, MA: Harvard University Press.

Monteith, Margo J. and Aimee Y. Mark. 2005. "Changing One's Prejudiced Ways: Awareness, Affect, and Self-Regulation." *European Review of Social Psychology* 16 (1): 113–54. https://doi.org/10.1080/10463280500229882

Monteith, Margo J., Steven A. Arthur, and Sarah McQueary Flynn. 2010. "Self-Regulation and Bias." In *The Sage Handbook of Prejudice, Stereotyping and Discrimination,* edited by John F. Dovidio, Miles Hewstone, Peter Glick, and Victoria M. Esses, 493–507. London: Sage.

Muldoon, Mark. 2002. *On Ricoeur.* Belmont, CA: Wadsworth.

Nadal, Kevin L. 2014. "A Guide to Responding to Microaggressions." *CUNY Forum* 2 (1): 71–76.

Nadler, Arie and D. Jeffrey. 1986. "The Role of Threat to Self-esteem and Perceived Control in Recipient Reaction to Help: Theory Development and Empirical Validation." In *Advances in Experimental Social Psychology* 19, edited by Leonard Berkowitz, 81–122. New York: Academic Press.

———, Samer Halabi, Gal Harapz-Gorodeisky, and Yael Ben-David. 2010. "Helping Relations as Status Relations." In *Prosocial Motives, Emotions, and Behavior*, edited by Marion Mikulincer and Phillip R. Shaver, 181–200. Washington, DC: American Psychological Association.

Nickerson, Raymond S. 1998. "Confirmation Bias: A Ubiquitous Phenomenon in Many Guises." *Review of General Psychology* 2 (2): 175–220.

Noddings, Nel. 2002. *Starting at Home: Caring and Social Policy.* Berkeley: University of California Press.

Nussbaum, Martha C. 1986. *The Fragility of Goodness: Luck and Ethics in Greek Tragedy and Philosophy.* Cambridge: Cambridge University Press.

———. 1995. "Objectification." *Philosophy & Public Affairs* 24, no. 4 (Autumn): 249–91.

———. 2000. *Women and Human Development: The Capabilities Approach.* New York: Cambridge University Press.

Ocampo, Josh. 2019. "How to Respond to Microaggressions as a Person of Color." *Lifehacker*, February 2, 2019. https://lifehacker.com/how-to-respond-to-microaggressions-as-a-person-of-color-1832531920

O'Neill, Onora. 1989. *Constructions of Reason: Explorations of Kant's Practical Philosophy.* Cambridge: Cambridge University Press.

Owen, M. M. 2018. "I and Thou. When We Encounter Another Individual Truly as a Person, Not as an Object for Use, We Become Fully Human: Martin Buber." *Aeon Magazine*, March 7, 2018. https://aeon.co/essays/all-real-living-is-meeting-the-sacred-love-of-martin-buber

Page-Gould, Elizabeth and Rudolfo Mendoza-Denton. 2011. "Friendship and Social Interaction with Outgroup Members." In *Moving Beyond Prejudice Reduction: Pathways to Positive Intergroup Relations*, edited by Linda R. Tropp and Robyn K. Mallett, 139–58. Washington, DC: American Psychological Association.

Parsons, Talcott. 1951. *The Social System: The Major Exposition of the Author's Conceptual Scheme for the Analysis of the Dynamics of the Social System.* New York: The Free Press.

Paton, Herbert J. 1964. "Translator's Preface." In *Groundwork of the Metaphysics of Morals* by Immanuel Kant. New York: Harper & Row, Harper Torchbooks.

Penner, Louis A. and Heather Orom. 2010. "Enduring Goodness: A Person-by-Situation Perspective on Prosocial Behavior." In *Prosocial Motives, Emotions, and Behavior*, edited by Marion Mikulincer and Phillip R. Shaver, 55–72. Washington, DC: American Psychological Association.

Phelan, Jo, Bruce G. Link, and John F. Dovidio. 2008. "Stigma and Prejudice: One Animal or Two?" *Social Science & Medicine* 67 (3): 358–67. https://www.ncbi.nlm.nih.gov/pmc/articles/PMC4007574/

Pittinsky, Todd L., Seth A. Rosenthal, and R. Matthew Montoya. 2011. "Measuring Positive Attitudes Toward Outgroups: Development and Validation of the Allophilia Scale." In *Moving Beyond Prejudice Reduction: Pathways to Positive Intergroup Relations*, edited by Linda R. Tropp and Robyn K. Mallett, 41–60. Washington, DC: American Psychological Association.

Popper, Karl. 1972. *Objective Knowledge: An Evolutionary Approach.* Oxford: Clarendon Press.

Porpora, Douglas V. 2015. *Reconstructing Sociology: The Critical Realist Approach.* Cambridge: Cambridge University Press.

Prasad, Monica. 2018. "Problem-Solving Sociology." *Contemporary Sociology* 47 (4): 393–98.

Ricoeur, Paul. 1981. *Hermeneutics and the Human Sciences: Essays on Language, Action and Interpretation.* Edited and translated by John B. Thompson. Cambridge: Cambridge University Press.

———. 1992. *Oneself as Another.* Translated by Kathleen Blamey. Chicago: University of Chicago Press.

———. 1998. *Critique and Conviction: Conversations with François Azouvi and Marc de Launay.* Translated by Kathleen Blamey. New York: Columbia University Press.

———. 2005. *The Course of Recognition.* Translated by David Bellauer. Cambridge, MA: Harvard University Press.

Rieff, Phillip. 1970. "Introduction." In *Human Nature and the Social Order* by Charles Horton Cooley (1902), third printing, ix–xx. New York: Schocken Books.

Roets, Arne and Alain Van Hiel. 2011. "Allport's Prejudiced Personality Today: Need for Closure as the Motivated Cognitive Basis of Prejudice." *Current Directions in Psychological Science* 20 (6): 349–54.

Rosenthal, Robert and Lenore Jacobson. 1968. *Pygmalion in the Classroom.* New York: Holt, Rinehart and Winston.

Rosenthal, Robert. 2003. "Covert Communication in Laboratories, Classrooms, and the Truly Real World." *Current Directions in Psychological Science* (Blackwell) 12 (5): 151–54.

Rousseau, George. 2006. "Curiosity and the *lusus naturae*: The case of 'Proteus' Hill." In *Curiosity and Wonder from the Renaissance to the Enlightenment*, edited by Robert J. W. Evans and Alexander Marr, 213–49. Gower House, UK: Ashgate.

Sampson, Edward E. 1999. *Dealing with Differences: An Introduction to the Social Psychology of Prejudice.* Fort Worth, TX and Orlando, FL: Harcourt Brace.

Sandel, Adam Adatto. 2014. *The Place of Prejudice: A Case for Reasoning within the World.* Cambridge, MA: Harvard University Press.

Sayer, Andrew. 2005. *The Moral Significance of Class.* New York: Cambridge University Press.

———. 2011. *Why Things Matter to People: Social Science, Values, and Ethical Life.* New York: Cambridge University Press.

Scheler, Max. (1913) 1970. *The Nature of Sympathy.* Translated by Peter Heath. New York: Archon Books. Original *Zur Phänomenologie und Theorie der Sympathiegefühle und von Liebe und Hass.*

Schroeder, Brian. 2006. "There's More Than Meets the Eye: A Glance at Casey and Levinas." *The Pluralist* 1, no. 1 (Spring): 98–103.

Schutz, Alfred. 1967. *The Phenomenology of the Social World.* Translated by George Walsh and Frederick Lehnert. Evanston, IL: Northwestern University Press.

———. 1970. *On Phenomenology and Social Relations.* Edited and with an Introduction by Helmut R. Wagner. Chicago: University of Chicago Press.

——— and Thomas Luckmann. 1973. *The Structures of the Life-World.* Vol. 1. Translated by Richard M. Zaner and H. Tristram Engelhardt, Jr. Evanston, IL: Northwestern University Press.

Shattuck, Roger. 1980. *The Forbidden Experiment.* New York: Farrar, Straus & Giroux.

Siegel, Daniel J. and Mary Hartzell. 2003. *Parenting from the Inside Out: How a Deeper Self-understanding Can Help You Raise Children Who Thrive.* New York: Jeremy P. Tarcher.

Simmel, Georg. 1907/1978. *The Philosophy of Money.* Boston: Routledge & Kegan Paul.

Simmons, Roberta G. 1991. "Presidential Address on Altruism and Sociology." *The Sociological Quarterly* 32 (1): 1–22.

Slote, Michael. 2007. *The Ethics of Care and Empathy.* London and New York: Routledge.

Smelter, Cara. 2018. A panel discussion at *Esse Quam Videri*, an art exhibition through the lens of disability. National Humanities Center, Durham, NC, September 20, 2018.

Smith, Christian. 2003. *Moral Believing Animals: Human Personhood and Culture.* New York: Oxford University Press.

———. 2010. *What Is a Person?* Chicago: University of Chicago Press.

Smith, Dorothy E. 1987. *The Everyday World as Problematic: A Feminist Sociology.* Boston: Northeastern University Press.

Sohn, Michael. 2014. *The Good of Recognition: Phenomenology, Ethics, and Religion in the Thought of Levinas and Ricoeur.* Waco, TX: Baylor University Press.

Stangor, Charles. 2009. "The Study of Stereotyping, Prejudice, and Discrimination within Social Psychology: A Quick History of Theory and Research." In *Handbook of Prejudice, Stereotyping, and Discrimination*, edited by Todd D. Nelson, 1–22. New York: Psychology Press.

Steinbauer, Anja. 2019. "The False Mirror: A Brief History of Prejudice." An editorial. *Philosophy Now 2019.* http://philosophynow.org/search?q=prejudice

Stets, Jan E. and Michael J. Carter. 2012. "A Theory of the Self for the Sociology of Morality." *American Sociological Review* 77 (1): 120–40.

Sue, Derald Wing. 2010a. *Microaggressions in Everyday Life: Race, Gender, and Sexual Orientation.* Hoboken, NJ: Wiley.

———. 2010b. *Microaggressions and Marginality: Manifestation, Dynamics and Impact.* Hoboken, NJ: Wiley.

———. 2015. "How Unintentional But Insidious Bias Can Be the Most Harmful." An Interview with Charlayne Hunter-Gault, PBS Newshour, November 13, 2015.

Sullivan, Shannon. 1997. "Domination and Dialogue in Merleau-Ponty's Phenomenology of Perception." *Hypatia* 12 (1): 1–19.

Swart, Hermann, Rhiannon Turner, Miles Hewstone, and Alberto Voci. 2011. "Achieving Forgiveness and Trust in Postconflict Societies: The Importance of Self-Disclosure and Empathy." In *Moving Beyond Prejudice Reduction: Pathways to Positive Intergroup Relations*, edited by Linda R. Tropp and Robyn K. Mallett, 181–200. Washington, DC: American Psychological Association.

Tarr, Zoltan, ed. 2011. *The Frankfurt School: The Critical Theories of Max Horkheimer and Theodor W. Adorno.* New York: Routledge.

Tavory, Iddo. 2011. "The Question of Moral Action: A Formalist Position." *Sociological Theory* 29 (4): 272–93.

Taylor, Charles. 1992. "The Politics of Recognition." In *Multiculturalism: Examining the Politics of Recognition*, edited by Amy Gutmann, 25–73. Princeton, NJ: Princeton University Press.

Terian, Sara Kärkkäinen. 1981. "Intimacy in Context: A Theory of Interpersonal Relationships." MA thesis, Western Michigan University.

———. 1984. "The Other Side of Good Samaritanism: The Helping Ethic in Judeo-Christian Ideology and Practice." PhD diss., University of Notre Dame.

Thomas, William I. 1923. *The Unadjusted Girl: With Cases and Standpoint for Behavior Analysis.* Boston: Little, Brown.

——— and Dorothy Swaine Thomas. 1928. *The Child in America.* New York: Knopf.

Treisman, Anne M. and Garry Gelade. 1980. "A Feature-Integration Theory of Attention." *Cognitive Psychology* 12: 97–136.

Tropp, Linda R. and Robyn K. Mallett, eds. 2011. *Moving Beyond Prejudice Reduction: Pathways to Positive Intergroup Relations.* Washington, DC: American Psychological Association.

Turner, Jonathan H. 2002. *Face to Face: Toward a Sociological Theory of Interpersonal Behavior.* Stanford, CA: Stanford University Press.

Wallace, Mark I. 2002. "The Summoned Self: Ethics and Hermeneutics in Paul Ricoeur in Dialogue with Emmanuel Levinas." In *Paul Ricoeur and Contemporary Moral Thought*, edited by John Wall, William Schweiker, and W. David Hall, 80–93. New York and London: Routledge.

Walsh, George. 1967. "Introduction." In *The Phenomenology of the Social World* by Alfred Schutz, xv–xxix. Evanston, IL: Northwestern University Press.

Weber, Linda R. and Allison I. Carter. 2003. *The Social Construction of Trust.* New York: Kluwer Academic/Plenum Publishers.

Webteam. 2011. "Academic exchange": Interview with Carol Gilligan. *Ethics of Care: Sharing Views on Good Care.* http://ethicsofcare.org/carol-gilligan/Interview, 07/16/2011.

Wheeler, Ladd, Edward L. Deci, Harry T. Reis, and Miron Zuckerman. 1978. *Interpersonal Influence.* Second edition. Boston: Allyn and Bacon.

White, Julie Ann. 2000. *Democracy, Justice, and the Welfare State.* University Park, PA: Pennsylvania University Press.

Witenberg, Rivka T. 2014. "Tolerance Is More Than Putting Up with Things—It's a Moral Virtue." https://theconversation.com/tolerance-is-more-than-putting-up-with-things-it's-a-moral-virtue-31507

Wojtyla, Karol (Pope John Paul II). 2008. *Person and Community: Selected Essays.* Series: Catholic Thought from Lublin. Translated by Theresa Sandok. New York: Peter Lang.

Wuthnow, Robert. 2017. *American Misfits and the Making of Middle-Class Respectability.* Princeton, NJ: Princeton University Press.

References

Zahavi, Dan. 2001. "Beyond Empathy: Phenomenological Approaches to Intersubjectivity." *Journal of Consciousness Studies* 8 (5–7): 151–67.

—— and Søren Overgaard. 2012. "Empathy without Isomorphism: A Phenomenological Account." In *Empathy: From Bench to Bedside*, edited by Jean Decety, 3–20. Cambridge, MA: The MIT Press.

Index

About the Author

Sara Kärkkäinen Terian, a native of Finland, has lived most of her adult life in the United States where she launched her academic career after living and working in six countries on four continents. She holds a PhD in sociology from the University of Notre Dame (IN) and has taught at several universities. Her publications include numerous articles and a book, *Basic Guidelines for Qualitative Research in Education* (2003). Now retired, she resides with her husband in Fresno, California.

www.ingramcontent.com/pod-product-compliance
Lightning Source LLC
Chambersburg PA
CBHW022326280326
41932CB00010B/1245